Wilderness Blues

T.B. Botts

Copyright © 2007 Good Catch Publishing, Beaverton, OR.

All rights reserved. Written permission must be secured from the publisher to use or reproduce any part of this book, except for brief quotations in critical reviews or articles.

This book was written for the express purpose of conveying the love and mercy of Jesus Christ. The statements in this book are substantially true; however, names and minor details have been changed to protect people and situations from accusation or incrimination.

All Scripture quotations, unless otherwise noted, are taken from the New International Version Copyright 1973, 1987, 1984 by International Bible Society

Published in Beaverton, Oregon, by Good Catch Publishing.
www.goodcatchpublishing.com
V1.1

Printed in the United States of America

To the best of my knowledge and remembrance, the stories portrayed in this book are true. I've changed the names of many of the people to avoid conflict. It is not my intention to embarrass or slander any of the persons mentioned. I've tried to record the history of my time at Game Creek as accurately as possible, without being offensive.

Sincerely, Tom Botts

Table of Contents

Chapter One	11
Chapter Two	37
Chapter Three	41
Chapter Four	52
Chapter Five	68
Chapter Six	76
Chapter Seven	83
Chapter Eight	91
Chapter Nine	99
Chapter Ten	101
Chapter Eleven	107
Chapter Twelve	111
Chapter Thirteen	118
Chapter Fourteen	124
Chapter Fifteen	134

Chapter Sixteen	144
Chapter Seventeen	149
Chapter Eighteen	152
Chapter Nineteen	155
Chapter Twenty	161
Chapter Twenty-One	169
Chapter Twenty-Two	172
Chapter Twenty-Three	179
Chapter Twenty-Four	183
Chapter Twenty-Five	187
Chapter Twenty-Six	194
Chapter Twenty-Seven	203
Chapter Twenty-Eight	219
Chapter Twenty-Nine	227
Chapter Thirty	230

Acknowledgements

Writing a book is not a one-person show. Without the help of a multitude of talented individuals, it would never get off the ground. Therefore, I would like to thank the following individuals.

First and foremost, I must thank the Lord. I'm not foolish enough to think that I could have done this on my own. Any skill that I may have, any talent or ability has come from you. Thank you.

Shelly Yandell. You read my first attempts to put into writing that which had only been in my mind for years. Without your encouragement, I might never have gotten beyond chapter one.

Chris Greenwald, librarian extraordinaire. Your patience with me while I struggled with computers borders on sainthood. The professionalism that you bring to your work is exemplary. You are an asset to the library, the school and the town.

Stephanie Harold. The hours you spent reading, correcting and guiding me through this process have finally borne fruit. Your generosity with your time and talents is greatly appreciated. Thanks so much, Steph.

My daughter, Jennifer, who read each chapter as it came hot off the press. Your laughter at the appropriate passages let me know I was on the right track.

My wife, Jan. Without your sacrifice, this book wouldn't have been possible. What more can I say? I love you.

Chris Budke, for the photograph that was used for the cover. You see the world through an artist's eyes. It was hard to choose just one picture. Thank you for sharing your skill with the camera. Great job, bro!

Finally, to all the folks who have called the farm at Game Creek home. I hope you can share with me the

Wilderness Blues

memories, both pleasant and not so much so, and maybe have a good laugh as we recall the time we spent together. Though we may be scattered to the four winds and may never see each other again on this earth, we will always be bound together by what we shared. God bless you and keep you.

Chapter One

I hate cold weather. I've never liked it – even when I was a kid back in Ohio – so it doesn't make much sense that I would choose to live in Alaska, a state known for its extreme weather. In retrospect, there isn't too much of my life that does make sense though, so moving to Alaska is no more foolish than anything else I've ever done, I guess.

I'm not too much of an adventure seeker. Most of my life was fairly uneventful, at least until the year I turned 24. In June of 1976, while the rest of the country was preparing to celebrate our country's 200th anniversary, I found myself loading our 1972 Pinto with as many of our worldly goods as it could possibly carry and embarking on a journey to Alaska. It would be, by far, the greatest adventure of my life.

I would like to share with you some of the stories that 10 years on an "end-time farm" in the wilderness of Alaska have provided me with. Not the usual encounters with grizzlies and blizzards, though there were certainly those. No, these are stories about an old lady with black panties, two-person outhouses, a farting accordion player and three-hour sermons. Though none of these would appear to be even remotely related, nonetheless, they are interwoven into the fabric that makes up the story of the farm and my 10 years of living there.

In 1974, the ship I was stationed on in Key West was decommissioned, and I was reassigned to another one located in Charleston, South Carolina. Jan, my wife, and I arrived totally unfamiliar with the area and not knowing a soul. I was certain that I didn't want to live on the naval base in the enlisted men's housing. I figured I saw enough of sailors on the ship without having them as my neighbors, so we went looking for a place off the base. We drove up and down the streets across from the naval base and in short

Wilderness Blues

order, spotted a real estate office. The man we met didn't have anything to rent in our price range but remembered the little bungalow behind his office was empty and called the caretaker. That's how we met Sandy.

Sandy Carson came right over and introduced herself. She was attractive, in her late 20s with large brown eyes and auburn hair that she kept pulled up in a ponytail that bounced when she walked. She smiled and stuck out her hand, and when she spoke, her voice was that of a Southern belle, someone who had been raised with good manners but not stuffy. I liked her immediately.

"Hi, ya'll, I'm Sandy. The cottage isn't mine, but I take care of it for my good friend, Nana. It's small but would probably be just right for a young couple like you."

We moved in, and two weeks later, I was on my way to the Mediterranean for a four-month cruise, courtesy of the U.S. Navy. When I returned, I found that my young wife had been attending church meetings in Sandy's home and seemed to be somewhat enamored with the people.

Sandy was really quite charming, and on several occasions, I'd observed her singing while performing menial tasks like hanging up the laundry or cleaning the car. It was behavior that I'd never observed before, and I found it intriguing. Eventually, I found myself spending almost every evening at her house, drinking iced tea and asking questions about God. I came to find out that she was an elder in her church, as was Amanda Harrison, her good friend and my landlord.

The church, as it turned out, was a tightly knit group of people made up largely of women and children who met together in each other's homes on Sundays. There were a few men who attended on a regular basis, but by and large, they seemed to be a needy lot. There was one old fellow who needed medication to help keep him lucid and a sandy-haired young man with a chin that could easily rival Jay

Chapter One

Leno, whose wealthy, overbearing mother forbade him to come to the meetings. There was also a Russian scientist who worked for the government in some capacity and dated one of the ladies in the group. He had really long hair that he couldn't seem to control and spoke with a strong accent. He was supposed to be some kind of genius, but I could never understand what the hell he was talking about.

There were a few fellows who came with their wives on occasion, men who I would consider normal for the most part. As soon as church was over, we'd step out on the front porch and light our smokes and talk about fishing or hunting. It felt good to be part of a group, away from the sailors and ships. As time went on, we spent more time socializing with the members of the church. The ladies frequently got together to have tea or clean house, though it seemed like Amanda's house was the only one that ever got cleaned.

Sometimes we'd all gather at John's Island for meetings. Sandy's sister and brother-in-law owned a small farm there, and often after church, a few of the men would take to the fields and hunt for rabbits or quail. We grew fairly close and though the church was the reason we came together to begin with, I wasn't totally happy about giving up my free time to attend.

The meetings dragged on for quite a long time, longer than any church I'd ever been to before, but sometimes we would have dinner afterwards and sit around and visit, which was always enjoyable. At one point, there were a couple of men who dropped in from out of town. Sandy said they were apostles and spoke pretty highly of them. They preached longer than normal, but much of what they said didn't make sense to me. Periodically, one of them would launch into a string of unintelligible words which really kind of threw me for a loop. Sandy explained later that he was speaking in tongues. It was unlike anything I'd ever been exposed to before and left me feeling pretty uncomfortable.

Wilderness Blues

It wasn't too long after the apostles left that the sermons took on an ominous air. A feeling of doom and gloom replaced the upbeat messages that I had been used to hearing. There was talk of end-of-the-world events, and a sense of paranoia seemed to permeate the room where we were gathered.

"People, God is providing a place for his people in the wilderness," Amanda said seriously. "Y'all need to hear what I'm saying. It won't be too long, and money isn't going to be any good. All hell is going to be breaking loose on this earth, and you need to decide if you're going to stay here or move on with the Lord. He's chosen a group of people to be a part of the first fruits company, and I believe with all my heart that includes us."

Most of what was said in the meetings went over my head, perhaps because I spent so much time dozing on the couch, but the one thing that did spike my interest was the talk of moving to Alaska.

There were several people attending the gatherings whose family members were vehemently opposed to both Amanda and the church group. Maybe they'd had dealings with her in the past, I don't know. It was all quite bizarre though, with people sneaking around, wives deceiving their husbands to attend the meetings and threats of lawsuits. I never knew that going to church could be such a traumatic event.

One night, I was asked to take Amanda and her youngest daughter to the airport to catch a midnight flight. They were on their way to Alaska.

"Don't let anyone know you took us here, darlin,'" she said in her matronly Southern voice. "I know this must seem strange to you, but there are people here who are against this Move of God."

Actually, the fact that people might be against the "Move," as the church was known, didn't seem strange to

Chapter One

me at all. What seemed strange was that Amanda was sneaking off in the middle of the night like some spy, but I didn't say that to her. Actually, I was kind of glad she was leaving. Initially, I kind of liked her, but the more I got to know her, the pushier she seemed.

As time went on, several other families from the church sold their homes, packed their belongings and headed north. Eventually, Sandy and her husband, Bill, and their two young children also left. I had grown quite fond of them and their leaving left a void. Though I'd never really given it much thought up until their departure, I started thinking more about Alaska. Within a year, we were to join them, though if I knew then what I know now, it never would have happened.

Tucked away on the northeast shore of Chichigof Island, about 40 miles west of the state capital of Juneau, lay the fishing village of Hoonah. The Tlingit Indians established Hoonah when the advancing glaciers forced them out of their settlements in Glacier Bay. While searching for an ideal location for a village, they lived in several spots in Icy Straits: Spasski Harbor on the southern side of the straits and Groundhog Bay along the area known as the Homeshore. Finally, they discovered Komtok Hon or Brown Bear Bay, later renamed Port Fredrick by Captain George Vancouver in honor of Adolphus Fredrick, son of King George III of England. There was an abundance of seals, deer and otter here, as well as salmon streams and a variety of berries. They had found what they had been searching for, a home for these displaced people. There were spruce and hemlock forests for homes and heat, food enough to sustain the whole village and a gently sloping beach for launching their canoes.

Down through the years, the village was known by a number of different names – Belltown, Gaud'ah'Kan, Hoonah Town, Hooniah, Hoonyah, Huna, Kantukan and

Wilderness Blues

Koudekan. In 1901, the Hoonah post office was established, thus giving the village its present name.

In the mid-1970s, Port Fredrick and the surrounding area were discovered once again, this time by a group of charismatic Christians who had a vision of a safe haven away from the carnal influences of the world. They felt that God had led them to this remote location to save them from the tribulation that was to come upon the world soon and to lead them on into perfection. While this may sound good on paper, the reality is quite a different story. Nonetheless, land was purchased and leased, and a few hardy individuals set out to build an "end-time farm" on the territory surrounding Game Point, a place about four miles south of Hoonah. The official name was Mt. Bether Bible Center at Game Creek. To the locals though, it was just the farm, and its inhabitants were "farmers" or "pilgrims."

It was to this remote fishing village in Southeast Alaska that our little green Ford Pinto plowed up the ramp of the Hoonah ferry terminal. As we reached the top, I rolled down my window, took a deep drag on my cigarette and pitched it out. Smoking was forbidden at Mt. Bether, so like it or not, I was going to quit …cold turkey.

As we pulled to the side of the parking lot, we were met by Ben Paulson, a friend from Charleston whose wife, Brenda, and mother-in-law, Amanda, were elders in the Move. Like me, he didn't seem to totally embrace the philosophy of the church but rather seemed to be going along for the ride, perhaps to maintain peace in the family.

Ben walked over, greeted Jan and the kids and shook my hand. He was on the short side and looked slimmer than I had remembered. He removed his baseball cap and ran a hand through his straight, thinning black hair.

"Well, I see you made it," he said. "Follow me, and I'll take you up to the dungeon."

Chapter One

Ben was a bit of a clown, always joking and goofing off, but there was something about what he said that kind of bothered me. That was an odd choice of words. I was already feeling pretty apprehensive about this whole experience of moving to the wilderness. Driving down the main drag didn't do much to lessen the anxiety. The primary road was nothing more than a narrow dirt lane with potholes you could float a boat in most of the time. The few days in the summer when it wasn't raining, the sun would come out with such intense heat that the mud would dry up like an adobe brick. The same westerly winds that brought relief from the constant drizzle and overcast skies would pick up the dust from the streets and hurl it dozens of feet into the air, so that anyone traveling by boat or plane could easily spot the town long before any houses became visible.

A long blast from the ship's horn interrupted my thoughts. I glanced in the rearview mirror and saw the ferry pulling away from the dock. For a few brief seconds, I contemplated turning around and waiting for the next one to arrive and just bagging this whole stupid idea. As it was, I kept following the car in front of me through the mud and ruts up to the residence that the farm maintained in Hoonah.

Traveling the five or six blocks from the ferry terminal to the town house was quite an eye-opening experience. Shoved against the side of the mountain in the narrow space between the road and the cliffs were a few rundown houses and a dilapidated trailer, the windows streaked with mud from passing vehicles. Across the road was the Wigwam Café, an A-frame building with the remnants of a boardwalk out front. Like the other structures on the beach, it rested on barnacle-encrusted pilings that appeared destined to give way at any minute. The splatter from the road was so severe that if the buildings had ever been painted, it was impossible to tell. We approached the downtown area and passed the

Wilderness Blues

abandoned hulks of several burned-out houses. One yard had an old school bus that looked like it had served as a temporary shelter for a while. A dirty blanket hung loosely in the broken windows, and a piece of rusty stovepipe protruded from the roof. Wild grasses, fireweed and nettles grew out through the front grill, and empty beer cans and liquor bottles were scattered across the ground surrounding the vehicle. In several lots, I noticed household appliances and outboard motors cluttered the lawns.

Off to my right, a ramp extended out into the bay where the floatplanes unloaded passengers and freight.

Beyond, the beach was littered with small fiberglass boats, their props raised, bows tethered to boulders or rotting engine blocks.

There were no sidewalks, so we frequently stopped to wait for pedestrians to move out of the way, which no one seemed to be in any hurry to do. The continuous stares that we received as we drove by left me feeling like an attraction in a circus parade. Adding to my discomfort, I noticed several bumper stickers that gave me the distinct impression that perhaps visitors weren't really welcome, at least not white visitors. Sayings like "Indian Power" and "Custer had it Coming" left me wishing that I had inherited more of my father's dark hair and skin tones. It was a relief when we pulled up to the Mt. Bether town house.

We arrived at a rundown residence that showed signs of having been painted white at one time. A couple of wooden planks spanned the gully between the road and the front porch like a gangplank on a ship. Salmonberry bushes engulfed the sides and back of the place and threatened to choke off the dim light that came in through the windows. For as bad as the house appeared, it didn't seem out of place. With few exceptions, most of the neighbors' homes looked as bad or worse.

Chapter One

There was an assortment of muddy boots on the front porch, so we took off ours and added to the pile. Ben opened the door, and we went inside.

The interior was as shabby as the exterior. When we entered the living room, I noticed a worn, green couch covered in a soft, knobby fabric that gave me the creeps. It looked sort of dirty, like someone had let their pets sleep on it. Beside it stood an ancient brass floor lamp, its shade mottled from age. The painted plywood walls were bare of any pictures or decoration; there was nothing to break up the drab appearance of the room, no candles or flowers or knick-knacks, none of the things that would give a home a warm feeling. It was dark and gloomy inside, and the air felt damp, like a musty basement. The scent of fuel oil mingled with the old house smell, and I wondered how anyone could stand to live here. Ben hadn't been wrong; the place did kind of feel like a dungeon.

We walked into the kitchen which was cramped and sparsely furnished. A small table and a mismatched assortment of chairs took up most of the space. On the left was an oil cook stove with a cast-iron top. In the archway between the two rooms was a stand for the telephone, a black rotary type – standard issue from Ma Bell in an era that had long since passed. I felt like I had stepped back in time 20 years. Perched on a shelf above the phone was a CB radio, the only means of communicating with the farm.

When we entered, Brenda Paulson, Ben's wife, greeted us warmly. "Uncle Tom, Aunt Jan, how nice to see y'all!"

We were in no way related, but the group in Charleston felt like it showed some respect to the grownups, without the formality of mister or missus, and they didn't want the kids to address adults by their first name.

Ben entered and asked his wife about lunch.

"We're having hot dogs," she replied.

Wilderness Blues

"Oh boy, hot dogs!" he exclaimed, rubbing his hands together. "That sounds great!"

I just assumed that his supposed excitement over something as mundane as hot dogs was another one of his gags. After all, who the heck would get all excited about having a hot dog for lunch? Watching him wolf down that weenie left me wondering if perhaps he'd skipped breakfast or something. Maybe he had to leave the farm early to meet the ferry.

While we were still eating lunch, a call came over the CB radio concerning transportation for my family and me. We needed to get out to Mt. Bether, and the only way to do that was to take one of the small skiffs across the four miles of water that separated the town from the farm. Arrangements were made for Jan and our two young daughters, Jennifer and Liz, to catch a ride out in one skiff, while I stayed behind and loaded up some of our clothes and other necessary items. I'd catch a ride out later.

We all walked down to a dock located in the center of town.

Several large white buildings straddled each side of the dock and rested on pilings that looked painfully inadequate.

A large metal sign on the tin roof declared it was the Thompson Fish Company.

We proceeded down a rickety wooden ramp to a float where a small boat was pulling up. Sitting in the stern was a handsome, stocky man with curly black hair and a shy smile that revealed teeth stained by years of black coffee and non-filtered cigarettes.

"It's Uncle Bill!" Jennifer shouted.

Bill Carson smoothly guided the skiff to the floating dock and grabbed a cleat to tie to. It was great to see another familiar face. After hugs and handshakes, Bill commented that the tide was going out, and if Jan and the girls wanted to save a long walk, they had better get going. Load-

Chapter One

ing up his precious cargo, Bill untied the skiff and roared off around the corner of Graveyard Island and out of sight, leaving the float I was on bouncing in his wake.

With my family in good hands and a few minutes to spare, I thought I'd take in some of my surroundings. Glancing down into the clear water, my eyes were drawn to movement. Ben Paulson followed my gaze and made a face.

"Tomcod," he said disgustedly. "They're all over the place. Not really good to eat, the meat is kinda mushy, but they're fun to catch when you've got the time. Most folks here just throw them back – if it's not a salmon or halibut they don't want it. Everything else is pretty much considered trash fish."

Well, trash fish or not, I was frantic to get a chance to wet a line in Alaskan waters. It was one of the primary reasons I had allowed myself to be talked into coming to an end-time farm to begin with – that and the impending doom that was soon to be coming upon us in these last days. In any event, my fishing rods were still stashed away in the trailer we'd towed from Charleston and would be unavailable for several days. The hundreds of tomcod seemed to be well aware of that fact as they lazily circled the pilings, scavenging scraps of fish from the processing plant above. I felt like a character in a Far Side comic with hundreds of fish right under my nose and no way to catch them.

The time finally came for me to catch a ride out to the farm. Bob Cramer, a lanky fellow with thick red hair and a serious expression, deftly maneuvered a large aluminum johnboat up to the floating dock where we were standing and started barking orders. I'd seen him once before at a church convention in Canton, Ohio, but I didn't really know anything about him, except that he seemed a little impatient right now.

"Come on, we don't have much time." Reaching into his front shirt pocket, he pulled out a small rectangular book

Wilderness Blues

and proceeded to study it. "According to the tide book, the high tide was about an hour ago – 16.4 feet. If we hurry, we can make it all the way up the creek. Let's get the rest of this stuff in the boat, and be careful how you load it. Distribute the weight evenly so we don't bottom out going up the creek."

Bob spoke like he knew what he was doing, and since I had no idea of what the plan was, I did what I was told. Nonetheless, the feeling of uneasiness that had settled into the pit of my stomach since our arrival remained. Loading the skiff quickly, I said goodbye to Paulson, and we raced off toward the farm.

Sitting stiffly in the bow of the boat, I felt the drum roll cadence of each wave on the water as we bounced over it. I had my first real opportunity to observe the surroundings of this beautiful place. Port Fredrick was carved out many years ago by the advancing glaciers of the ice age.

When they receded, they left behind a deep-water bay surrounded by heavily forested mountains that spill into the inlet. With the snow-capped peaks, lush green forests and vast expanses of clean, clear water, it was by far the most beautiful place I'd ever seen. However, its beauty was tempered by the ever-present gray clouds that hung low over the horizon, lending a gloomy air to the place.

As we zoomed past a small island, Bob waved his hand to get my attention. Pointing to a stretch of grassy beach, he shouted, "I shot a brown bear right there a couple of days ago."

Having just met Bob Cramer, I didn't know if he was telling me a tall tale to try and impress the new guy or if indeed he had actually shot one of these coastal grizzlies.

Seconds later he proclaimed, "We're going to be eating it tonight."

I have to say, this was most unusual table fare. Hot dogs for lunch and brown bear for supper was not at all what I

Chapter One

had envisioned when the subject of meals on the farm entered my mind. All the movies that I'd ever seen where farm folk were sitting down to dinner involved fried chicken or roast beef, mashed potatoes and corn on the cob. Television farmers knew how to eat. I had yet to see a movie where the farmer comes in from the fields and sits down to a hefty plate of bear meat; but this was Alaska, and for all I knew, that's what folks up here eat. In any event, supper was still awhile away so there wasn't much sense in worrying about it now. Bear meat for supper – this was going to make for some interesting letters to the folks.

We passed by the island and took a left, searching for the passage that led up through Game Creek. Bob maneuvered the small boat skillfully around mid-channel boulders and trees, deposited after last spring's floods, all the while fighting the rushing current as the tide receded.

We finally arrived at our destination, a natural landing where the creek took a sharp bend as it flowed out to the bay. Several cottonwood trees were leaning toward the water, their roots exposed in the damp mud where the streambed had shifted with the last winter thaw.

A few men and older boys met us with wheelbarrows. Bob jumped out of the boat and grabbed the bowline to keep the boat from drifting.

"Grab that line from the stern, and hold us in place," he commanded.

One of the boys retrieved the rope from the boat, and another jumped in and started passing my stuff to the waiting crowd. In short order, the skiff was unloaded. Bob stepped in, and using a paddle, shoved off from the shore. In a few brief seconds, he disappeared around a bend in the creek. I watched until he was gone and turned to the business at hand.

Wilderness Blues

Following after the line of wheelbarrows down the sawdust path, my ears were assaulted by a deafening, high-pitched buzzing sound.

"What's that noise?" I asked the kid in front of me.

"Sawmill!" he shouted back.

The path we were on changed from sawdust to a boardwalk made up of two rough-cut wooden planks laid side by side and nailed to a cross piece on the ground. The constant traffic had worn the wood smooth, and the continual rain made them incredibly slippery. I noticed that everyone on the boardwalks walked with a kind of skating motion to propel himself forward. It was the only way to stay on two feet. Once in a while, someone would get a new pair of neoprene boots, 16-inch Uniroyals or Xtra Tuffs, standard fare for Southeast Alaska, and for a few days, he would proudly walk the boardwalks with the confidence that the extra tread would bring. Within a short time though, the tread would wear down, and they would be back to doing the boardwalk shuffle.

On the short trip from the creek to my new home, we passed several cabins. Unlike the log cabins farther north, these were rather plain in appearance: two-story, boxy-looking dwellings built with the same rough lumber that the boardwalks were constructed of. Plastic covered the window openings, and the crude doors had been slapped together with lumber from the mill. It appeared that the cabins had been built in haste and served function, not fashion. Not a drop of paint had been laid to any of the homes, and far from looking rustic, they had the look of neglect. Crusty black creosote rimmed the tops and dripped down the sides of the metal stovepipes that protruded from the roof of each building. The white wood smoke that rose from each one hung low in the air, trapped by the dense atmosphere. The smell was stifling, almost oppressive, and I wondered how Jan would fare here with her asthma.

Chapter One

My family and I were finally united in front of a small travel trailer, the kind that you might rent to go on vacation.

"I guess this is where we're staying," Jan said.

"What the hell?" I replied. "I thought we were going to have a cabin or an apartment or something. Crap, this isn't big enough for four people to live in. If I had known it was going to be like this, I never would have come here!"

She gave me a glare that could freeze water, and when she spoke, her voice was low and tense.

"Look, we spent 10 days getting here; everything that couldn't be used here is either stored at my parents' house or sold. We've used all our money just getting here so please don't start bitching now. You haven't even been here a day yet."

What she said was true. As I looked around, the reality of my situation really hit me. I was outside an 18-foot travel trailer that was soon to be my home, surrounded by dozens of people, many of whom I didn't know, in the middle of a Christian community in the wilderness of Southeast Alaska. As if that weren't bad enough, I hadn't had a cigarette for hours, and the withdrawal symptoms were killing me. The real icing on the cake though, was what my wife had said about having spent all of our money to get here. My God, we're stuck! I couldn't leave if my life depended on it. Waves of despair washed over me, and for the umpteenth time that day, I wondered what I had gotten us into.

Around 5:00 someone rang a dinner bell – the old-fashioned triangle type like you used to see in Western movies. We had the pleasure of meeting up with Sandy and Bill and were invited to eat supper with them in their cabin.

Walking inside, I was a little surprised to see how small the living space was. Actually, I was shocked. The moderately sized cabin, which could accommodate one family comfortably, was divided into four apartments, with three families and a group of single ladies sharing the space. Like

Wilderness Blues

all the rest of the buildings, it was solid wood from the base to the ceiling. I glanced at the floor and noticed sawdust in the large gaps between the planks. It served as insulation in lieu of the commercial fiberglass type. Much of the interior paneling was cracked and knotholes pockmarked the surface, testimony to the hot, dry heat from the woodstove. However, Sandy had managed to make a lovely home in the most unpleasant of conditions. The windows had red and white gingham curtains hanging, with a tablecloth to match. The bed in the corner was neatly made and had little pillows trimmed in lace propped on it. The place was as neat as a pin, and although it was cramped, she exercised her Southern charm to make us feel perfectly welcome. Within minutes, she placed a plate in front of me piled high with rice and gravy and some kind of green leaves that were supposed to pass for salad, I guess. After blessing the food, Sandy suggested we dig in before it got cold; it was good advice.

After the first bite it was apparent that if you let this stuff cool off, there was no way you'd be able to choke any of it down. Bob Cramer had been telling the truth; he had indeed shot a brown bear, and we were most certainly eating it for dinner. The gravy that topped the rice was littered with large chunks of bear meat. I don't remember when I'd ever tasted anything so nasty. After a few minutes of poking at the mess on my plate, I made some excuse about not being too hungry and left, hoping I might find some crackers or ketchup packets or something left over from the trip. One thing was painfully clear: with no cigarettes to console me, and an empty stomach, I was in a world of hurt with no relief in sight.

While Jan stayed behind with the kids and gossiped with Sandy, I took off down the slippery boardwalk toward the creek, trying not to think of the emptiness in my guts. The sawmill was finished operating for the day, so the only sound I could hear was that of the creek running and the

Chapter One

call of some varied thrushes or telephone birds. They got their name from the noise they make, which sounds a bit like a phone ringing. Rounding the corner, I saw a few kids standing on the bank of the creek, casting for trout. A few hours before, the water had been spilling over the bank.

Now the creek was rushing by, and it had dropped by at least six feet. Standing nearby on an outcropping of rocks, I noticed Carson's son, Doug.

"What are you up to, Bubba?" I asked, happy to see yet another familiar face.

"Hey, Uncle Tom! My lure is snagged on the bottom. I can see it there, but it won't come loose, and my dad won't let me wade out into the creek to get it."

Sure enough, just a few yards away, sparkling in the current was a brilliant gold spoon. Wanting to make a good impression on the kid, I offered to try and get the lure loose for him. Taking the rod, I proceeded to try every trick that I knew in an attempt to loosen it, but all to no avail. Finally, not wanting to lose the little guy's respect, I opted to go in after the blasted thing; after all, it was right there, just staring me in the face, practically inviting me to come and get it. So I did – or at least tried to. Sitting on the gravel bar, I peeled off my tall rubber boots and socks and prepared to go be a hero. With pants rolled to my knees, I plunged my bare feet into that stream like I was taking a walk in the park. Nothing in my life had ever prepared me for the shock of stepping into that snow-fed creek barefooted. The cold penetrated all the way to my throat with a pain that robbed me of my breath. This water had to be colder than the snows that fed it. After taking about four steps into the liquid ice, retreat was the only thing on my mind, not an easy task. The rocks that paved the creek bed were rounded like cobblestones and were packed so tightly together that there was no place to get a foothold. To make matters worse, the creek was rushing by so fast that I could barely stay upright on the

Wilderness Blues

slippery stones. Tottering like a drunken fool, I worked my way back to shore. Finally, defeated, I returned to the riverbank.

"Sorry, Bubba," I mumbled. "It's stuck, and I just can't get it loose." I handed him his rod and sat on the wet bank to put my socks and boots back on my throbbing, red feet; so much for playing the hero today.

From the moment I had stepped foot on this place, nothing had gone right. I had no cigarettes, I was hungry, Jan and I had already had a fight, my new home, which incidentally was located in the middle of an Alaskan rainforest, was designed for temporary camping trips, not full-scale living, and to top it all off, I had publicly humiliated myself in front of a bunch of kids. What the hell – it was time to go "home" and try to salvage something of what remained of the day.

Following the path back to camp, I cautiously approached the boardwalk. I didn't want to throw my back out by slipping on the stupid walkway my first day. As I walked along, I was struck by how light it was. 10:00 p.m. and it was still brilliant enough to read. This was going to take some getting used to. My mind didn't want to believe the clock. With the sun not setting until midnight or later, there was no reason to stop working on outdoor projects due to darkness. Thunderation – I could stay up half the night fishing if I wanted to. You don't even feel tired when it's still light out. Unfortunately, kids felt the same way. Parents had problems putting their children to bed; it wasn't dark enough to go to sleep.

By the time I stepped inside, Jan had the girls bedded down for the night. It had been a long day, and everyone was exhausted. The camper we were assigned to had a propane heater, which was on when I arrived. Though it was summer, there was a damp chill in the air that penetrated my clothes and left me feeling cold.

Chapter One

We finally hit the sack ourselves, lulled by the pleasant sound of a soft rain gently falling on the metal roof above us and the telephone-like call of the varied thrushes drifting through the woods we were surrounded by.

I awoke to sunlight streaming through the windows of the trailer. A quick glance at my watch revealed that it was just past four in the morning, but already I could see my surroundings easily.

Sometime during the night, the rain had stopped and the thrushes had fallen silent, replaced by a new, more demanding sound. At the first sign of daylight, the ravens started their search for food. These large, black birds resembled crows on hormones. They had huge, pointed beaks and intelligent eyes that could spot food from far away. Their obnoxious calls echoed back and forth throughout the camp, and their massive wings made a whooshing sound as they chased each other through the spruce branches as if they were playing tag.

However, it wasn't the early morning light that awoke me or the noise of the ravens. No, it was a sensation – one that I hadn't experienced for many, many years, not since I was just a young lad. What had awakened me so early was the discomfort of wet bedding. The bed wasn't just damp, it was soaked! What the …did I pee the bed? Was that possible? Could I have been so exhausted that I failed to heed the pleading of my bladder during the night? Could this be a side effect of nicotine withdrawal? While I was still contemplating all this, another thought entered my mind. Maybe Jan wet the bed, poor gal. She was going to be really embarrassed. Moments later, while I was still wondering how all this was going to play out, Jan started stirring. Her eyes fluttered open as she lay on her back, staring at the ceiling. Sitting up, she exclaimed, "The roof leaks! There's water all over everything – the ceiling, the floor, the walls, everything!"

Wilderness Blues

Sure as the world, she was right. Everything was wet, but not because of a leaky roof. The culprit was the propane stove. When the heat came in contact with the cold metal of the trailer, condensation occurred. In essence, it was raining inside my home. While it was a great relief to find out we hadn't peed our beds, we were still going to have to deal with the condensation problem if we were going to stay in the trailer. This was not a good way to start the day!

After finding some dry clothes and getting the girls dressed, Jan set off down the path towards the cabin that housed the camp kitchen. All the meals on the farm were prepared here. There was an enormous cast iron cook stove inside, fueled by wood. On top was an aluminum pot suitable for feeding large numbers of people like at a school or military barracks. The cook ladled out the contents into four melmac bowls, and Jan shuffled down the boardwalk with our breakfast on a tray. It all seemed quite surreal. Overhead the ravens and crows squawked, no doubt waiting for someone to slip on the path and spill their tray. The birds were much less picky about their chow than I was.

When Jan returned with our breakfast, I was dismayed to see that once again my preconceived ideas about farm meals were misplaced. Instead of the eggs, sausage and biscuits that I had imagined, there were four steaming bowls of cornmeal mush and four slices of slightly stale, homemade wheat bread. It was hardly the breakfast of champions. There wasn't even any coffee. How anyone could be expected to work on so meager a meal was a mystery to me, however, having eaten so little in the previous two meals, I wasn't about to pass this up. Grumbling, I quickly scarfed down the meal in front of me and started eyeballing the kids' food. Apparently, they were hungry, too, so there was nothing left for me to clean up.

Chapter One

My stomach was growling as I stepped outside to join the men and boys by the boardwalk for a work assignment. At that moment, I would have killed for a cigarette.

I sauntered over to Uncle Bill, one of the few people I knew, and smelled the unmistakable aroma of tobacco smoke clinging to his clothes. Bill was still smoking! Somehow he managed to get away with it. Maybe having a wife who was an elder gave him an edge. I started to say something when Bill looked at me with upraised eyebrows, smiled and shook his head. Though it was too hard to hide, he didn't want to discuss it, at least not in front of this crowd. I found out later that it was no secret that Bill was still smoking, but all attempts to confront him were futile. Eventually, they just gave up trying.

After being introduced to everyone, work assignments were handed out. I was directed to go to the fields to work with Brother Robert, a soft-spoken, boyish-looking fellow with pink cheeks and curly brown hair. His speech had a distinct, smooth, Southern draw that, for some reason, irritated me.

"Brother Tom," he smiled, "maybe you could load up those hoes into the wagon, and we can start out to the fields. We have a lot of work to do today."

"Just plain Tom," I said, bristling. I hated being called brother. Looking around, I noticed that Robert, myself and the lone black person on the farm, a fellow named Jason, were the only men assigned to the fields; all the rest of the folks were women and children.

We loaded the tools into a horse-drawn wooden wagon, and Robert grasped the reins, directing the horses like a stagecoach driver from the old West. Leaving the camp, we started off down the uneven road towards the fields. We bounced over rocks and plunged into ruts in bone-jarring jolts that left my head aching. Up front, on the driver's seat, Sandy was talking and laughing with Robert and Jason, en-

Wilderness Blues

joying the companionship of her fellow field workers. Consigned to the bed of the wagon with the women and children, I felt a slight twinge of jealousy.

A dense forest of tall spruce and hemlocks gave way to a thick stand of alders, which bordered the road we were traveling. Stretching off to the right was the mudflats over which my family traveled yesterday, only now it was low tide and the water had receded, leaving behind a vast expanse of mud and small tidal streams.

The wagon rounded a bend, and I found myself awestruck by the view that lay out before me.

Directly in front was lush, green grassland that undulated in the wind like a flag. Beyond were the wooded hills and valleys that rose and fell like a roller coaster. Further yet was the majestic beauty of Ear Mountain. On sunny days, the snow covering the rounded twin peaks is so brilliant it hurts your eyes. Long strings of mist lay in pockets, giving it a magical appearance.

While I was still taking in the scenery, the wagon jolted to a stop in front of a freshly plowed strip of land. "Here we are," Robert called out. "Everyone grab a tool."

I'd never had much experience in a garden but figured it couldn't be too difficult to plant a few cabbages. I should have known better. The ground was riddled with rocks that were embedded in the sticky mud like bricks in mortar. Bending over to install the cabbages was backbreaking labor, and I had visions of going through life unable to stand up straight, like the rice farmers of the Orient.

Clawing at the ground with my hoe, I noticed the slight morning breeze had ceased altogether, and the air hung still and heavy with moisture. With no wind to deter them, a cloud of ravenous gnats descended on us, hungry for blood. They flew into every orifice they could reach and camped out on our foreheads and earlobes, chowing down. I cursed and swatted at them with hands that were gritty with mud,

Chapter One

but it didn't help. For every one that I killed, two more showed up. A fine mist started to fall that I thought might chase off my attackers, but they didn't seem to mind a bit. If anything, it refreshed them – a little something to help wash down my blood.

Right when I thought things couldn't possibly get any worse, someone started singing. Soon others joined in. After awhile, it became apparent that I was the only one who wasn't singing. Great, this was just what I needed! I was stuck in the middle of a cabbage patch with the hallelujah choir, getting bled dry one painful drop at a time by a swarm of starving insects. It just doesn't get any better than this – or so I thought.

I was still complaining to myself when Jason pulled up in the wagon. He had gone into camp to get our lunch. There was to be no reprieve from the bugs or rain; we were going to eat out in the fields. He stepped down, carrying a huge rectangular pan covered with a checkered cloth.

"Family," Robert spoke, addressing the crew, "Brother Jay brought us some lunch, so we should probably take a few minutes and eat before it gets cold."

I was all for that. The little bit of breakfast that I'd had earlier was long since used up. As Jan used to say, I was so hungry, I could eat the butt end out of a rag doll.

After a blessing had been said, one of the ladies started dishing out the meal. In my short life, I'd seen some strange things, but this took the cake. On the plate in front of me was a brown and yellow quivering blob of goo that, for all the world, made me think of a cow pie. Looking around at my fellow diners, I noticed that no one seemed to be in any hurry to eat. From off to the side I heard, "What is it?"

Jason slowly looked up from his plate. "The kitchen ladies said this was bear liver mush," he stammered.

Bear liver mush! Who the heck …what kind of mind could conjure up such a nasty concoction? I was so hungry

Wilderness Blues

that I finally tried a bite. Yuk! It tasted as bad as it sounded. I was quite certain that if I remained at Mt. Bether, I was sure to starve to death, or at the very least, go nuts.

Sometime after lunch, the eldership sent word that they wanted to see me. They were the governing body/ religious leaders of the camp. I was about to experience my first elders' meeting. Though I was feeling a little apprehensive, I was nonetheless happy to get away from the hordes of bloodthirsty insects that had plagued us all day.

I met up with Jan, and we walked over to the Carson cabin where the meeting was to be held. We stepped inside and were assaulted by a blast of hot, dry air from the small woodstove in the corner, quite a contrast to the cold drizzle I had been in all day. The entire eldership was there: Sandy, Amanda and Brenda from the Charleston group, Barbara and Larry Boryslaw from the farm at Ware, Massachusetts, and John Borelli from I don't know where – New Jersey, I think. We looked for a place to sit in the cramped apartment and finally settled in on one of the beds. It was stifling in there, and I wondered if I might pass out before the meeting was over.

"Ya'll come on in," Sandy said warmly. "Can I get you anything, a cup of coffee or tea?" As she scurried around the small space preparing the drinks, she spoke again in that Southern drawl that I so loved to hear.

"First, we wanted to welcome ya'll here," she said smiling. "We missed you so much. God has been so good to us here, and we're just happy to share this blessed place with you. Things here are a little different than they were down in Charleston. We have to depend on each other more, and there has to be some order to keep things running smoothly."

"What do you mean?" I asked.

Larry piped in before Sandy could answer. In his 30s, with dark hair and eyes that he averted when he spoke, he

Chapter One

had a somewhat cocky attitude that turned me off right away.

"Of course, you know that there is no smoking or drinking on the farm. This is a Christian community, and we believe that the body is the temple of the Lord. The ladies and girls all have to wear dresses or skirts, nothing too short. Modest dress is required here. You'll be expected to keep your hair trimmed, and you'll have to shave off your mustache. Many of the young men here came from the hippie movement, and we view facial hair as a sign of rebellion."

Periodically, he looked up with a crooked little smile, apparently amused by what he'd said and checking to see if anyone else found him funny. He continued on with a list of do's and don'ts that would have made Moses proud, but I wasn't listening anymore.

When I left the meeting, my mind was reeling. This was more reminiscent of my time in the Navy. The last thing I wanted to do was come under a bunch of rules and regulations. Charleston hadn't been like this at all. I felt a little betrayed that neither Bill Carson nor Paulson had ever bothered to mention the strict rules that were in place here before I came. As we walked down the path towards our little trailer, a feeling of panic started to rise within me. I already hated this place, but for at least the time being, I had no place else to go.

Chapter Two

The only good thing that I could see that came from that meeting with the elders was a change in job assignments. I was able to convince them that I would be more useful elsewhere, hoping that they would place me with Uncle Bill and the building crew, but no such luck. Instead, I was assigned to the sawmill. At least it was located in the perimeter of the camp, so we should be able to stop and eat lunch inside. Also, unlike the field crew, the mill consisted of an all male group.

The next day, after another meager breakfast of hot cereal and a slice of bread, I headed down to my new work assignment. After greeting my fellow laborers, I was introduced to the sawyer, Pete Warner. Standing before me was a man in his mid-30s of medium build that belied his strength. Covering a shock of black hair was a greasy, billed cap stenciled with the logo of some chainsaw company. He wore thick, black-rimmed glasses that propped up his bushy eyebrows, and he had a bit of a wild look in his eyes that became more pronounced when the saw was running. A leather apron hung down over his plaid, flannel shirt, which was covered in sawdust and splinters. When I was introduced, he looked up briefly, shook my hand and continued sharpening the saw blade, intent on the job in front of him.

The mill was dark, noisy and dirty. A few bare light bulbs dangled from the rafters and did more to add to the gloom than dispel it. The place smelled of wood smoke, diesel and freshly cut spruce. Logs were stacked on a ramp behind the blade and were wrestled into place when needed by two men with pee-vees, wooden-handled tools with sharp metal spikes and hinged claws.

The saw blade was as tall as a man and covered in sharp, removable teeth. In front of the blade were several sets of

Wilderness Blues

rollers for moving the lumber down the line to the edger, where the bark was cut off. Afterwards, it was passed to another man to be separated according to size.

Nothing went to waste. The slabs, large bark-covered planks from the outer log, were used to build roads. The smaller stickers, or edges, were cut to size for use as firewood. Even the sawdust was put to use, some as animal bedding, some to cover the mud in the roads and the majority as insulation for the various building projects, especially the root cellar.

Sometime during the morning, the saw struck a rock that was embedded in a log. The mill was shut down so Pete could sharpen the blade. I wandered over to where the rest of the crew was standing and struck up a conversation.

"Doesn't anyone ever take a break here?" I asked. "You know, have a cup of coffee or something?"

Three faces looked up at me expectantly. "Normally, Pete doesn't take any breaks. Sometimes when he's really going good he doesn't even stop for lunch, but if you have some coffee or something, we can go snag some while he's busy with that blade."

Much to everyone's disappointment, I had neither coffee nor snacks. I discovered then that anything above and beyond the three meals the farm served were my responsibility to purchase, whether it was coffee, snacks, even powdered milk for the kids. If I wanted it, I bought it.

The very mention of snacks started a flurry of conversation. One of the young men from the Ware group started talking about life on the farm in Massachusetts.

"We used to go to the bakery and get all the three-day-old bread and pastries and feed the pigs," he said. "Sometimes, we'd hide behind the barn and eat these cream-filled donuts that they tossed. We had to keep an eye out for the elders though; if we got caught, we'd get in trouble."

Chapter Two

"Trouble? Why would you get in trouble? You were just going to feed them to the pigs, anyway."

"Yeah," he replied, "but it had something to do with feeding the flesh man and not dying to self. I'm not sure exactly, but we didn't want to get called in before the elders."

What he had said was unsettling to me. It was apparent that the group from the Ware farm had been subject to much more law and order than what I'd been exposed to in the Charleston body. They were a whole different creature than what I was used to.

Though what he had said was troubling, it took a backseat to the rumbling of my stomach. The mention of pastries, even three-day-old ones, was enough to set my mind to fantasizing about turnovers and cupcakes, delights that I may never see again if I stayed here.

Food was always on our minds, and whenever a group of men got together, it was the primary topic of conversation – meals we had eaten or would like to eat. After a few days on the farm, even the chow that I had whined about in the Navy sounded good. In the weeks to come, we would endure cabbage leaf soup, stewed nettles and radish pudding. Good Lord – radish pudding! I'd never heard tell of such a thing in my life. How anyone came up with that bright idea is beyond me, but somehow they did. The scary part was I was so desperate for something sweet that I actually enjoyed it.

Work at the sawmill was tedious and grueling. The green lumber was heavy and difficult to maneuver in the tight space, and often there were pockets of sticky sap that smeared our clothes and clung stubbornly to our hands for days at a time, leaving dark streaks that refused all efforts to remove them. The noise from the diesel and the whine of the saw as it ripped through the boards was deafening, even with earplugs, so conversation while the mill was running

Wilderness Blues

was fruitless. Any communication with my fellow workers was limited to a few hand signals, so my mind had lots of time to wander, which it did freely, over a landscape of angry thoughts and pools of depression.

The constant drizzle and clouds were fertilizer for my dark thoughts, and the hunger in my belly reinforced the anger I was feeling. What the hell was I doing here? I wanted to leave, to just escape from this nightmare, but I couldn't; I had no money, and if the elders were to be believed, I was right where God wanted me. He was dealing with me, and the flesh man was rebelling, but the spirit was growing stronger if I would just yield to him; all that aside, leaving would be akin to a spiritual death sentence. I just wish I had known that before I came to the farm. I might have taken my chances with all the tribulation that was going to be coming upon the world. At least I could have gone to McDonald's a few times before all hell broke loose.

Chapter Three

After I'd been on the farm a week or so, I felt like the walls were closing in. Day after day, the weather had been gloomy. Grey clouds and drizzle were our constant companions, and it was starting to take a toll.

Frivolity was scarce amongst my fellow workers. I can't remember anyone telling a joke or just being silly. The only ones that seemed to be having any fun were the really religious folks, who I couldn't relate to at all. Periodically, one would come waltzing down the boardwalk, whistling or singing some song from the meetings or shouting "Hallelujah" or "Thank you, Jesus" or some such thing. I always wondered if they were really that happy or if it was all for show. There was a lot of pressure to look Godly there. In any event, I was having a hard time relating. To make matters worse, I was suffering from nicotine withdrawals, and I was hungry all the time. I wasn't having fun, and I needed to get away for a while. I had to get into town and soon, before I was a complete basket case.

Trips into town were a little hard to come by. John Borelli, one of the elders, was in charge of the farm boats, and any transportation arrangements had to be made through him. I don't know what qualifications he possessed that made him more capable of running a boat than anyone else. I think the main criteria were that he was an elder, and he liked going into town. In fact, he was such a regular customer at one of the stores that he had his own coffee cup hanging in the office. He claimed to be a good will ambassador for the farm, a job I would have gladly assumed.

There seemed to be a concern at the time that we might be corrupted by worldly influences if exposed to them, so the less time spent away from the farm, the better. I found it strange that a member of the eldership, who made trips into

Wilderness Blues

town on a daily basis, could somehow keep from being impacted by all the apparent evil that was there, but I never voiced my concerns.

I mentioned to John that I needed to get into town and immediately got the third degree.

"What do you need to go to town for, Brother Tom?" he asked. He was soft-spoken and had a slight Italian accent, though he had been in America for quite a few years.

"I've got to go pick up some more of my stuff," I said happily, not realizing that a trip to Hoonah required a certain degree of necessity that could only be determined by a member of the eldership.

"Tell me what you need, and I'll get it for you."

That wasn't the answer I expected, so I tried again.

"No, I need to look through the trailer and see what we need and what we don't; I better go in and check it out myself."

"If you would let me know what you're after, I'm sure I could find it, Brother," he insisted.

I was starting to see where this was going and decided to get a little more forceful. "Look, John, I've got to get into town. I want my stuff, and there are other things that I need to do."

"Brother Tom, what things do you have to do that I can't take care of for you?" he asked softly.

My mind raced for an excuse that would be acceptable. I wasn't a prisoner here. How could they keep me from leaving? As a feeling of panic started to creep up into my throat, a thought came to mind.

"I've got to open a bank account!" I shouted, happy to have thought of a reasonable need. "And I need to talk to my folks." Whoa, a double header. I was on a roll. Reluctantly, he agreed to let me travel with him the next day.

The day dawned bright and clear, and it seemed as if a spell had been broken. Throughout the camp, there seemed

Chapter Three

to be a cheerfulness that had been noticeably absent. The sunshine made everyone feel better. The anger and frustration of yesterday was replaced with a feeling of euphoria as I hurriedly finished my breakfast and ran out to meet up with John and the other travelers. There was a carnival-like atmosphere amongst us, and though they didn't express it, I felt like everyone was as happy as I was to be leaving for the day.

Talking and laughing, we crossed the slippery planks of a giant wooden float that protruded out onto the mudflats. It was constructed of huge logs that were lashed together by thick steel cables that formed a raft of enormous proportions. More logs had been fitted to make an A-shaped boom that towered above the raft.

Rusty cables and pulleys dangled from the cross piece and lay in stiff piles on the deck. It had once been used to yard trees out of the woods before roads crisscrossed the landscape and the only logging was that which was accessible from the beach. Having served its purpose, it was donated to the farm and now served as a launch platform of sorts, extending far out into the mudflats. It was a formidable structure and was the first thing anyone noticed when approaching the farm.

We stepped down into the sticky muck and started across to the beach on the other side. With a sliding, skating motion, we tried to stay on top of the mud which threatened to suck the boots off our feet if we stopped for more than a few seconds. Almost everyone had lost at least one encounter with the flats.

The soft ground was a challenge, and it was exhausting to keep moving across it. The heavier ladies seemed to be especially vulnerable. They usually lagged at least a few steps behind the rest of the group, and it wasn't unusual to hear a yelp and look back to see some poor soul bent over at the waist with all four appendages stuck in the mud. It usually

Wilderness Blues

took two men to rescue the unfortunate gal, and in most cases, one or both boots were wrenched off in the attempt. It made for great conversation the next day as long as the ill-fated victim wasn't present. One of the larger gals refused to cross the flats at all after a couple times of being stuck.

Once across the flats, we encountered a different problem. The small stretch of beach between the water and the woods was covered with barnacle-encrusted rocks of all sizes. Cursing under my breath, I struggled to keep up with the others, huffing and puffing. Years of smoking had taken its toll. Barnacles crunched under our feet, and I hoped I wouldn't end up with a hole in my rubber boots. Near the water's edge, the hollow, whip-like stems of brown bull kelp were scattered along the beach, drying in the sun.

"Watch out for the kelp," John called back. "It's really slippery – don't step on it." Of course, the warning didn't come until I had already stepped on it and did a back-wrenching dance while trying to stay erect.

After a five-minute walk on the shore, we came to a reef that jutted out into the bay. It appeared as if we were at a dead end. However, up in the woods, well above the high tide line, was an aluminum canoe, large enough to carry three or four people.

"Grab the back, Brother," John commanded, as he hoisted the front of the canoe up. We walked, jerking and stumbling down the sloping beach, tripping on rocks and banging the sides of our legs with the canoe as we made our way to the water's edge. I discovered some time later that it was easier to pack it overhead alone than to try to keep in cadence with another person.

We paddled out to a wide, heavy plywood boat, some 20 feet long, with deep sides. It was anchored about 30 yards offshore. He called it a jitney, but I believe it was better known as a power scow, a short, beamy workboat used to stretch out seine nets for salmon. It was seriously under-

Chapter Three

powered with only a 50-horse outboard on the back. It was slow but could pack a heck of a load. John stepped into the boat and moved some things around before going to the stern to start the engine. After several tugs on the starting rope, the engine roared to life, and he untied from the anchor and motored into the beach to pick up the other travelers.

With everyone on board, he backed up and turned the bow toward town. I stood in the stern, trying to stifle the smile that was working its way across my face. I didn't want John to think that I was going to derive too much pleasure from this excursion.

Looking into the clear water below, I could make out the soft, umbrella-like bodies of white and red jellyfish undulating in the current. All around us dozens of dog, or chum salmon, jumped, and I desperately wished we could stop and fish for them.

We finally pulled up to the floating dock that belonged to Hoonah Seafoods, the largest of the three local stores. Up until recently, it served as a crab cannery and employed dozens of townsfolk. Now it primarily provided fuel and groceries and a little hardware to the residents of town.

Stepping out onto the float took a bit of daring. The wet boards were slimy from the constant rain, and there were soft spots and holes in the planking, but that wasn't the only challenge. One side of the float was partially submerged so that it tilted at about a 20-degree angle. Just stepping out of the boat took a certain amount of skill and luck. Adding to our discomfort was the audience we had. Gawking at us from their perches at the Down the Beach Bar, a number of patrons peered through the picture window waiting, perhaps to see if we would provide them with some entertainment. However, everyone managed to get onto the dock safely, and as a group, we worked our way up to the store.

Wilderness Blues

Over the years, I observed that whenever a group of farmers came to town, we always seemed to cluster together, moving en masse like a herd of sheep and always in a hurry. None of us walked at a normal pace; it's as if we were competing in some marathon, rushing here and there. The tide was certainly a factor in this behavior; it seemed we were always trying to catch it at a favorable point, but I can't help but wonder what the locals thought. I'm sure we looked the part of aliens with our bright yellow rain suits and life vests, the women in their skirts with jeans underneath, rushing through town like their backsides were on fire.

Walking inside the store, we all went our separate ways, though there weren't too many places to go. The aisles were very narrow and cramped. It reminded me of the corner market where my family shopped when I was a kid, in the days before supermarkets were the norm. I found the cooler where the soda pop was located and grabbed one. Then on to the potato chips and down the aisle where the Twinkies were. Though I wasn't a big fan of Twinkies, I knew that if I didn't indulge in one, I would never be able to get them out of my mind. Besides, I wanted to go back to those jerks on the sawmill crew and tell them how much I had enjoyed eating mine. On the way to the checkout stand, I snagged a red delicious apple. A week on the farm with no fresh fruit and not so much as a cookie for dessert had left a serious void in my sweet tooth. Watching my fellow travelers check out their purchases, I saw that we all felt the same.

There was an unspoken rule at the time about eating things that would be considered unhealthy like pop, candy or chips. I don't think it had so much to do with not being good for you. It was more a matter of fulfilling the lust of the flesh. We were supposed to be dying to self, not satisfying all of our fleshly, carnal desires. However, it never seemed to stop anyone from indulging themselves on their infrequent trips to town. The primary objective seemed to

Chapter Three

be to consume all your snacks before returning to the farm, something that was surprisingly easy to do.

I left Hoonah Seafoods and marched down the muddy street, licking the last bits of flavor from an ice cream bar stick. I stopped at the bank to open up a checking account with the last few dollars we had left. We really didn't need a checking account – there wasn't anything to buy on the farm and darn little in town – but I wanted to be able to use the excuse of having to go to the bank so I could get off the farm again. The bank building, like the other six or seven buildings that made up downtown Hoonah, was in dire need of repair or at least a good paint job.

Leaving the bank, I wandered right next door to the See's Greenwald Store. I walked up the few concrete steps, and as I passed through the doorway, I felt as if I had walked into the past. The wooden floor creaked as I entered, and little puffs of dust stirred as my feet disturbed the dry mud that had been tracked in from the streets all day. The homemade wooden shelves were sparsely stocked, and it was hard to see the merchandise in the back part of the store where bare incandescent bulbs provided the only light. I looked around, grabbed another pop and walked across the street to the only other store in town, L. Kane's.

The sign out front said "Established in 1893," and it had the appearance of having been around that long, though I believe the building may have burned down in 1944 along with most of the rest of the town.

Like the other two stores I had frequented that day, it was dimly lit and poorly stocked. One local fellow had complained that this was the only store he knew of, and that if he were accidentally locked inside overnight, he would be just as hungry in the morning.

The aisles were barely wide enough to let two people pass and then only if they turned sideways, unless one of them happened to be heavy, in which case you had to wait

Wilderness Blues

for them to move. There was a small refrigerated meat case beside the counter, but the only thing inside was a package of slimy, dark, semi-green hamburger and some black pieces of stew meat — at least that's what the label said it was. Apparently, fresh meat was hard to come by, and the owner didn't want any to go to waste.

Leaning on a scarred, wooden counter was a short, gray-haired native gal with coke-bottle-thick glasses and jowls that shook when she talked. She was standing beside an ancient brass cash register that had large round buttons with numbers on them. When the buttons were pushed, the price would appear in a glass window at the top, and a bell would ring when the drawer was opened. It was definitely an antique, like the cashier.

I chose a couple of candy bars from the limited supply available and asked what I owed. Instead of telling me, she proceeded to ask about the farm.

"How many of you folks are out there now?" she asked haltingly.

"I'm not real sure," I replied.

"You know, we used to go there for hunting and fishing until you people came. It's real good fishing ...and clams. Good clam digging on the beach."

"Yeah, well, is that right?" I was at a loss for words.

"You know, I love the Lord. My daughters and their children all go to church every Sunday, a Pentecostal church, sometimes on Wednesday, too. We're glad you people are there. Too much parties here – too much young people drinking. Maybe you folks can show them how to be."

"Hmm, yeah, well maybe," I stammered. I was starting to get a little nervous. Partially because we were talking about God, whom I knew very little about, and partly because a line was starting to form behind me. At any moment, I was afraid that someone would tell me to shut up and get the hell out of the way, but it never happened. The

Chapter Three

cashier, seemingly oblivious to the line stretching out behind me, continued to ramble on, and the folks in line carried on their own conversations, not seeming to notice the delay.

I was finally able to break away after making up a story about having to catch the boat back to the farm. Armed with my candy bars, I worked my way out through the squeaky door and into the muddy street.

It was time for lunch up at the town house, and as stuffed as I was from all the junk food I'd eaten that morning, a week on the farm had taught me that when the opportunity to eat arrived, you didn't pass it by. I walked up a hill and onto a path that led to the town house. The farm had sent in some of the same fare that they were eating out there, so I decided to pass on lunch and took advantage of the fact that I was in town to call my folks. That was the only other really good excuse that a person could use to get off the farm. Making a phone call home was something only you could do yourself.

There was a four-hour time difference between Ohio, where my family lived, and Alaska, so I had to keep that in mind whenever I called. 10:00 p.m. here would be 2:00 a.m. there.

At the time, satellite communications were still in their infant stage, so there was a several second delay between the time that you spoke and the time that the party at the other end heard you. To complicate things, there was an echo, so that you could hear everything you said over the phone at the same time the party you were speaking to heard it. Picking up the phone and dialing my folks' number, I heard my mom answer on the third ring.

"Hello."

"Hi, Mom," I said, only to hear, "Hi, Mom," back.

In the receiver at the same time, she said, "Well, hi, Tom!" A few seconds lapsed while I tried to comprehend what was going on.

Wilderness Blues

"Hello?" she said again.

"Yeah, I'm still here, Mom. Do you hear an echo when I talk — echo when I talk?"

"No," she said hesitantly.

I was finally able to convey to her what was going on with the phone, having to use satellites and the time delay. I let her know that there was no phone on the farm but to feel free to call, and I could come to town and call her back. After assuring her that Jan and I and the grandkids were fine (which wasn't totally true if mental state was considered), I hung up. It was somewhat confusing and outright frustrating to carry on a long distance conversation. Like so much else here, using the phone was a learning experience.

While it was great talking to family back home, it left me feeling lonelier than before we spoke. My parents didn't understand why we felt the need to live thousands of miles away, depriving them of their only grandchildren, and I hadn't done a very good job of explaining what we were doing, because, frankly, I didn't really know myself.

It was finally time to go back to the farm and leave all the pleasant delights Hoonah had to offer, so as a group, we sauntered down the hill, stopping once again at each store for a final snack as we worked our way back to the boat. We loaded up, untied and started plowing our way back "home." Everyone in the old jitney was quiet on the return trip; maybe they were feeling bloated from the junk food we had all consumed, or perhaps they, like me, were already cooking up some scheme that would allow them another trip into town.

Chapter Four

Life on a wilderness farm in Alaska is, if nothing else, unique. There were challenges around every bend. In those early years, when the farm was just getting established, we encountered many of the same trials that the pioneers of yesteryear faced, and I'm sure a few that they didn't.

One of the greater challenges was using the outhouse. Having grown up in an average American family, where indoor plumbing was available, the only time I used an outhouse was on those rare occasions when we would visit a state park for the day on a family outing. When the urge hit, you would reluctantly march to it, relieve yourself and rush out, holding your breath the whole time. It never occurred to me that one day an outdoor john would be a normal part of my everyday life.

Like so much else at Game Creek, going to the potty was an adventure. There were two outhouses within the camp, both built to accommodate two people at once – I'll explain more about that in a minute. They were elevated so that all the waste was deposited in two empty 55-gallon oil drums with the tops removed. That made sense. Being in a rain forest, the water table was very near the surface, so any hole that was dug would immediately fill with water, rendering it useless. The solution was to raise the structures to accommodate the drums, which were sitting side by side on a heavy wooden sled. When they were somewhat full, whoever was assigned the task was supposed to hook up the tractor, oxen or horses and haul the sled out to a pit in one of the fields and dump them. As you can imagine, it wasn't one of the more coveted jobs. Human nature being what it is, the task was put off as long as possible. The end result was that the barrel would get dangerously full.

Chapter Four

Hauling them through the camp on the corduroy road took the skill of a tightrope walker. Taking a corner too fast or catching a high spot in the road …well, you can imagine the mess. Finding volunteers to take on the potty barrel duty was always difficult. It was a true test of Christian love. You had to have the love of God if you were willing to do that job. There used to be a saying on the farm about preferring your brother. I know that I certainly preferred that my brother haul out those barrels.

In terms of efficiency, the double barrel design for the outhouses was probably a wise thing. If you're hauling crap anyway, you may as well get rid of twice as much at the same time. What didn't make sense about the twin stalls was that they were unisex. There was no men's or women's room, so to speak. On many occasions, I would be answering nature's call when I would hear footsteps on the boardwalk as someone approached the privy. As they climbed the steps, I would have a feeling akin to panic. I should mention here that I was somewhat timid and easily embarrassed. I never knew if I should rush through what I was doing and run out the door before the person beside me finished or if I should sit quietly and hope the person next door wasn't a talker. (Several people had no qualms about talking to the person next door while sitting on the john.)

The problem with sitting quietly was that it made you feel like a pervert. The walls separating the two stalls were painfully thin. A mere one inch of wood was all that came between you and your neighbor. Every sound from start to finish was readily heard with stereo-like clarity. Believe me, the temptation to head to the woods for relief was ever present.

Toilet paper – let me say a few words about toilet paper or the lack thereof. Let's face the facts. I would venture to say that most of the world gets by just fine without it. It's a luxury that we Americans enjoy; however, on the farm,

Wilderness Blues

unless you could afford to buy your own, you had to use what was provided. The *Juneau Empire*, the local newspaper, proved to be sufficient as toilet paper. It had the added advantage of giving you something to read while you were occupied. There was no television on the farm and only a few radios, so news from the outside was hard to come by. One way to get caught up on world events was to run to the potty. Unfortunately, the news could be days or even weeks old, depending on when the newspapers were picked up from town. Another problem was the "toilet paper" was cut into four-inch squares, so you might be reading an interesting article about the cold war or a drought somewhere when the narrative would stop in mid-sentence. Sometimes by piecing together enough squares, you could get the full report; of course, that all took time. In most cases, the rest of the story was in the bottom of the potty barrel.

I can't really recall right now who was in charge of the toilet paper detail, but it runs in my mind that either one of the young, single women or perhaps one of the elderly ladies used to gather a group of children and sit down with the newspapers and blunt scissors and cut it into squares. After a sufficient stack was made, it was gathered up and delivered to the brightly decorated coffee cans that served as the toilet paper receptacles.

I don't want to brag, but when it comes to toilet paper, I'm a bit of an expert. Having spent 10 years on the farm, I feel more qualified than many people on the subject. With authority, I can declare that not all toilet paper is created equal. For instance, magazines were down near the bottom of the list, in terms of preference. While they were better than no paper at all, they would be ranked only one step up from leaves. Most magazines have glossy pages, which meant they had a tendency to slide right over the affected area with almost none of the desired results. A few of the more studious types of people realized that by crinkling the

Chapter Four

magazine pages you could more or less increase their absorbency. It was not uncommon to be seated in the outhouse and hear the person next door crunching up the toilet paper they were using, sometimes with great vigor.

Newspapers may have been much more absorbent, but they were also very rough on tender skin. They had the added disadvantage of leaving behind the newsprint on your hands after handling. It was a good reminder to wash your hands after a session in the outhouse.

Every now and then, someone would get hold of some patterns, the kind that are used to make dresses and shirts if you're handy with a sewing machine. They were pretty soft and felt good but were painfully thin. A person could easily go through the makings of a size 10 jumper in just one sitting.

Of course, the commercial brands of tissue paper were by far the best if you could afford to buy them. Even they were not totally exempt from problems though. One fellow I knew complained that his "ass looked like a cotton field" after using a popular brand known for its softness. I guess the ideal toilet paper would be softer than sandpaper and more absorbent than magazines but not given to leaving behind more than it removes.

While I'm on the subject of outhouses, I'd like to relate to you several stories that involve them. Although there are probably dozens of stories involving the privy at Game Creek, these few stand out in my mind.

There was a young elder named Jeff who volunteered for potty detail. The barrels were really full and in need of removal. He hadn't been too long out of the Army, so he should have known better than to volunteer for anything.

Jeff always wore brilliant yellow raingear outside, rain or shine. He had a strong, forceful voice that could be heard from far away and a take charge kind of attitude that wasn't totally unpleasant. I kind of liked the guy. For an elder, he

Wilderness Blues

wasn't too bad.

The common practice when on potty detail was to first secure whatever means of locomotion you were going to use to move the barrels. Most people didn't hesitate to relinquish the horses or tractor, even if they were involved in a very essential project. Dumping the potties was a pretty important job, and if someone was willing to do it, by all means, don't hold them back!

After pulling up to the outhouse, the saint in charge of the detail was supposed to knock on both doors to make sure they were empty, rope off the front to keep people out and proceed to the rear of the building so he could remove the privacy panel and access the barrels. Well, I'm not sure if Jeff got distracted or if he just plain forgot to check for occupants, but in any event, he got an eyeful. Sitting inside on one of the seats was Sister Jeri T. Now, Jeri was a fairly hefty gal and not given to moving too quickly, and since there wasn't any place to go anyway, under the circumstances, she just sat there and hollered. Looking up, Joe got a shot of a full moon and proceeded to start speaking in tongues at the top of his lungs. The commotion alerted the whole camp. Had they remained calm, no one would have been the wiser and the whole thing would have blown over, but there are some situations where maintaining your composure just isn't possible. Both parties exchanged numerous shouts of "Oh my God!" and after hurriedly replacing the back panel, Jeff left the area and Jeri returned to her duties. It was chalked up to a learning experience for Jeff, as well as the rest of the potty barrel haulers, and of course, provided the camp members with something to laugh about for a long time, though never in the presence of Sister Jeri.

This next story involves the only other really heavy woman on the farm. I never really thought about it at the time, but being fat on the farm was kind of a paradox. There was no way that anyone who ate only the meals on the farm

Chapter Four

could be overweight. Anyway, this gal, Sister Linda, was fat. She seldom walked further than she had to. Her primary route was from her home to the tabernacle for meals or meetings, a distance of roughly 75 feet. I don't know if the main outhouse was too far for her to walk to, or if she just liked her privacy, but she had her husband, John, build her an outhouse right outside their cabin.

Linda and John had a son, John Jr. One day, Junior went hunting and had the good fortune of shooting a deer. For reasons unknown to me, he hadn't dressed it out in the woods, which is the common practice. Young John was a wee bit lazy, so instead of taking the entrails to the compost pile, he figured he'd just dump them down the family outhouse hole and save himself a few steps. Of course, he didn't bother to tell anyone what he'd done. It wasn't a big deal, at least not to him. Later that evening, his mother slowly worked her way across the snow-covered boardwalk in the dark, balancing the kerosene lamp in her hands while trying to keep from slipping. After relieving herself, Linda happened to glance into the privy hole on her way out. There, floating amongst the waste was the guts that Junior had discarded earlier that day. She had no idea that they were deer entrails; she thought they were her own. Fully convinced that she had just crapped her guts out, she proceeded to scream for her husband. In time, Junior confessed, though he didn't see what the big deal was because no one had said not to do it. Eventually, Sister Linda's nerves calmed down, and Junior came out from under the bed where he had been hiding.

Using the outhouse was only one of many adjustments that had to be made. While it was a bit inconvenient, and at times outright uncomfortable, it wasn't the greatest hardship we faced. There were so many difficult challenges that I can't really say which the worst was.

It's hard for most folks to imagine what life would be

Wilderness Blues

like without the many modern conveniences that we take for granted, for instance, indoor plumbing. I'm not talking about toilets here, I mean turning on a faucet and having water come out. For the first few years at Game Creek, we didn't have that luxury. All the water that was used for cooking, cleaning, laundry, baths or drinking was hauled by hand.

Aside from the potty barrels, water hauling was probably one of the least desired jobs. The chore fell primarily to one man. His name was Seth. He had a freckled face, a small mouth with thin lips and thick, wavy auburn hair that looked like it had been pasted on his head; it never seemed to move no matter how breezy the weather was. (Jan says it's because he never washed it.) Whenever I saw him, I thought of Howdy Doody, a puppet from a kids' show back in the 50s. Aside from his duties as the camp water bearer, he also had the distinction of being the accordion player at the church meetings.

Anyway, Seth took on the burden of supplying the whole camp with water. To help him in this chore, someone had devised a wooden yoke that he placed on his shoulders. From this yoke, he could hang two plastic five-gallon buckets, one on each side, for balance. He would deliver water to each residence in the camp, carefully dumping the buckets in clean plastic garbage cans and returning to the creek to fill up again. Occasionally, demand outstripped supply, and after the daily men's meeting, we'd all have to grab buckets and head to the creek. It was quite a chore, and I was always glad when we were done. For the life of me, I don't know why we didn't just fill a bunch of buckets at once and deliver them in a cart, but we didn't. Things at the farm were seldom done in the most efficient manner. At times, it seemed like we made an effort to do things the hard way.

Game Creek was a fast-moving, snow-fed body of fresh water, but on exceptionally high tides, it would fill all the way to the camp with salty or brackish water, making it im-

Chapter Four

possible to use for drinking. It was home to three species of salmon and several species of trout. In the summer, the creek would fill up with spawning fish, which would eventually die and leave their rotting carcasses scattered along the banks and collecting in pools until the rains came and washed out the remains. I can't remember if we collected rain from the rooftops or continued to drink from the creek. I just remember the water tasting like bleach from the copious amounts used to purify it. I guess it worked – no one died from drinking the water, although there might have been a few bouts of intestinal distress attributable to it.

No one was exempt from the hardships, including the ladies. In many ways, they had it more difficult than the men. Laundry was an especially demanding chore. Each married woman was responsible for her family's laundry, while the single gals were assigned to do laundry for the single men. I can't really recall the exact order of things, but it runs in my mind that a day was set aside each week for washing clothes. It usually took the entire day, too. Because there was no electricity, there were no washing machines. Clothes were placed in a round, galvanized washtub with a washboard, just like Grandma used to use. The work was slow and painful, especially in the winter.   W a s h t u b s were set up on the tabernacle porch outside, and water was hauled from the creek. On cold winter days they had to skim the ice from the washtub before washing. Several pots of water were kept on the stove to help cut the chill, but the effects were only temporary. Soon the ladies would be back to plunging their hands into water that was only a few degrees above freezing. I distinctly remember Jan standing on the tabernacle porch doing the family laundry with hands as red as beets. I felt like a creep for getting my clothes dirty. I believe it was several years before a laundry house was finally built so the ladies could have the luxury of working indoors.

Wilderness Blues

Bathing was also a bit of a challenge. In the early years, a shower was out of the question. Laundry tubs served a dual purpose as bathtubs. Water was heated and the kids sat in the tub and bathed. Sponge baths were the norm for the adults. Though we lived in a rain forest and were surrounded by water, it wasn't wasted. It was too hard to come by.

Of course, each cabin had to be heated, and because there were no roads to town, we couldn't just call up the fuel company and place an order. Besides, we were supposed to be self-sufficient, so we had to use what was available, which was wood. Each cabin had a wood burning stove, which ran 24 hours a day. There was also the kitchen stove where all the meals for the entire camp were cooked. Needless to say, supplying wood for the entire camp was a full-time job.

In the early days, a crew was sent up the bay to fell trees. Usually the crew was made up of single men who, to the best of my knowledge, had no experience with logging whatsoever prior to moving to the farm. Nonetheless, they took to the woods with chainsaws and wedges and other tools necessary to drop the huge spruce and hemlock that grew right down to the beach. I was always a little jealous of the logging crew. It wasn't because of their willingness to endure hardship or their strength but because they were given store-bought food. Before every trip they were loaded up with peanut butter and jelly, eggs and coffee and I'm not sure what all else. I just knew that they were eating better than I was. Of course, the flip side of that was that they slept in a yurt, a kind of wooden tent set up on the beach. There was no way to dry their clothes, and small mouse-like rodents called voles invaded their food cache.

After a sufficient number of trees were felled, they were rounded up into a raft and towed to the farm.

Chapter Four

The better quality logs were bucked to size and taken to the sawmill, while the butt ends and lesser quality logs were left on the mudflats in a corral to prevent them from escaping when the tide came in. On the very large tides, when the water came well up the shoreline, several of the fellows donned chest waders and moved the logs up higher onto the beach. After the tide receded, a crew went out with chainsaws to buck the logs. The blocks of wood, or rounds, were then loaded onto a cart or sled and hauled to the cabins, where it was split and stacked in a woodshed. It was hard, dirty work, made all the worse by the rain and bugs in the summer and the snow and ice in the winter. We never got caught up with the firewood because there were so many other jobs that needed to be done.

Being assigned to the firewood crew was actually rather satisfying for me. It was gratifying to feel the heft of the chopping maul as I lifted it high overhead and brought it crashing down on a block of hemlock, the hollow thunk sound of a well-placed blow, the crack that appeared on the face of the wood as it yielded to the hardened steel. After the first few minutes, jackets and sweatshirts were tossed aside, allowing more freedom of movement and cooling our overheated bodies.

Occasionally, a blow would be misplaced, and instead of striking the wood with the head of the maul, the handle would hit it and send shockwaves all the way up your arm. It wasn't that uncommon of a thing to happen, and those of us who had mauls with hardwood handles could often pick them out of a group by the size of the gouge in the handle.

With few exceptions our firewood was wet. Well, not just wet – saturated would be more like it. The logs rested on the mudflats in front of the tabernacle and rose and fell with the tide twice a day. Some sucked up so much water that they actually sank. Many blocks were so waterlogged that they would spray with each blow of the maul – some-

Wilderness Blues

times with such force that anyone close by would be splashed repeatedly with the foul-smelling stench of mud-flats water. Of course, there wasn't much heat produced by wet wood – mainly it would just sit in the stove and sizzle. The common practice was to set enough wood around the outside of the stove so that in the morning it would be dry enough to burn.

That reminds me of another story. Shortly after we had arrived, one of the ladies asked if I would start the stove in the tabernacle; it had gone out. Well, how hard can it be to start a fire? I had gotten in trouble with the cops once when I was 12 for starting a fire back in the woods near my home. I may not know much, but I could at least start a fire in a woodstove! Finding some damp kindling and newspapers, I started to work. I noticed there was also a coffee can nearby with Blazo written on the outside. Blazo was the brand name of the fuel that we used for our Coleman lanterns. I assumed it must be there to help light the wet wood. After filling the stove with kindling and paper, I doused the whole mess with Blazo and lit a match. Orange flames shot out of that stove like a rocket ship at liftoff! Slamming the door shut, I listened with some satisfaction as the wood inside crackled. After less than a minute though, the crackling stopped. I sat there wondering what the heck was going on. Slowly, cautiously, I opened the door and peered inside. Charred wood and burnt paper lay smoldering on the bottom. A stream of blue-white smoke came wafting out. "What the ..." Striking another match, I tossed it in. Flames shot out for the second time, lighting up the room and singeing my eyebrows. Man, a guy could get hurt doing this!

Speaking of fires and firewood brings to mind night watch duty. In the early days, it was decided that for safety reasons there needed to be someone up all night to make sure no one's cabin caught on fire and also to get the kitchen stove started in the wee hours of the morning. Since

Chapter Four

the stove was only needed for meals, there was no reason to keep it going after supper. This not only saved wood, but it kept the ladies who slept overhead from roasting to death. Even though the wood was always damp, the stove put off quite a fair amount of heat. This was mainly because the firebox was exceptionally small, so all the wood that went into it had to be reduced to kindling size, which burned fast and hot.

    As luck would have it, I was assigned night watch duty with a man named Gregg, a baby food salesman prior to getting involved in the farm. Now, maybe luck had nothing to do with it. Perhaps it was the way that the more spiritual folks said it was …that God was testing me. That I was "going through the fire." (That was a phrase that was used quite a bit around the farm. Anytime someone was having a bad day, which in my case was every day, they were said to be "going through the fire.") There was a feeling that all the tests and trials were somehow going to make you stronger spiritually; that for reasons that God alone knew, we were being "refined like silver in the furnace of affliction." Well, that may be true. No doubt there is something to be learned in all trials and tribulations, and I'm sure that there was some spiritual fruit produced because of them. However, I'm straying from my story. As I was saying, I was assigned night watch duty with Gregg, probably one of the most incompetent men ever to grace an end-time farm. I'm sure in his chosen field of work he performed quite nicely, but here he was totally out of place. Tall and thin with neatly combed hair, he made frequent sarcastic remarks that were punctuated with a mean little laugh at the end. As I recall, he was the only person on the farm that complained more than me. It was readily apparent that manual labor was not his cup of tea, and on more than one occasion, he delegated his work to one of the young boys. I believe that he was eventually assigned to work as a supervisor for the younger crowd. Be-

Wilderness Blues

ing somewhat weak and unwilling to share in the workload, he wasn't very popular with most of the men. Even the women seemed to avoid him. In an environment where everyday life was so dependent on everyone pulling his load, there just wasn't room for slackers.

Obviously, there hadn't been much thought involved when the two of us were given the responsibility of keeping the camp safe for an entire night, and not just for one night, but for the whole week!

The first night started off okay. I met Gregg downstairs shortly after midnight. There was only one Coleman lantern between the two of us and that happened to be mine. That meant we'd have to stay together all night. Hmm…I wasn't sure I liked that idea too much. I just hoped he wasn't afraid of the dark. If I had to take a leak, I didn't want him following me just because I had the light.

For the first few hours, things went pretty well. We made the rounds of the camp. There were no lights on in any of the cabins, and the only sounds were of the rain dripping off the metal roofs and the occasional hiss of raindrops spattering against the hot cap of the lantern. Several hours into the night, while we were in the tabernacle reading, light started to pulsate, growing dim and then bright.

"The lamp is running out of fuel, Gregg," I said. "We have to get on down and refill it before it goes out." Working our way out into the blackness of the night with our only source of light rapidly dimming, we shuffled as quickly as we could over the slimy boardwalks, struggling to maintain our balance. The filling station was no more than two 55-gallon drums set on their sides in wooden cradles with spigots attached; one contained kerosene, and the other had Blazo. I got the fill cap off the lamp and put it under the spigot just as the light went out.

"What great timing," I thought. My feelings of good fortune were short lived though. It hadn't occurred to me to let

Chapter Four

the lantern cool down for a few minutes before filling, so I didn't. I filled that puppy right up to full and beyond. In the darkness, I couldn't see how full it was, so a little of that Blazo spilled right out and came in contact with some hot part of the lamp with the obvious results. Of course, I set the damn thing down and proceeded to catch the sawdust under the fuel barrels on fire. I was having visions of being blown to pieces, and I wasn't any too happy with the idea of sacrificing my life for the farm.

Silhouetted against the flames, Gregg started dancing around, his thin arms and legs flailing up and down.

"Fire! Fire!" he screamed shrilly.

"Shut up!" I yelled. "You'll wake up the whole camp!" It would have been totally embarrassing to have some of the more capable men come down in the middle of the night and rescue the guys who were supposed to be keeping the camp safe. Kicking and stomping the flaming sawdust while I alternately cursed and prayed, the blaze gradually subsided. The whole incident only lasted a few seconds, but it left me breathless and shaken up. There was no doubt in my mind that God had intervened in what could have been a colossal disaster.

Later, after lighting the lamp well away from the fuel drums and buildings, we sat down to eat a snack. It was the best part of being on night watch. There was never much – a piece of bread or maybe two if you were lucky and a little peanut butter in a bowl. Sometimes there would be a raw egg that you could cook after the kitchen stove was started. That was nice to have, but it meant you had to wait until the stove was hot enough to cook on, usually around 5:00 a.m. It made for a dreadfully long night. By the time morning rolled around, my guts were usually pretty much in an uproar.

Around four in the morning, Gregg and I decided to light the kitchen stove. So far my luck with wood stoves had

Wilderness Blues

been pretty non-existent; tonight was going to be no different. We walked into the cabin where the kitchen stove was located. It was a monster of a thing, about eight-foot long and three-foot wide, solid cast iron. No doubt it weighed a ton. I was sure glad I wasn't around when it was installed. We shoved the firebox full of newspapers and kindling that we'd chopped outside earlier. We didn't want to wake up any of the ladies that were sleeping upstairs. The kitchen cabin housed most of the single gals in the camp, including a group of elderly ladies known as the Thirty-Niners. Striking a match, we waited in anticipation. For some unknown reason, the fire didn't want to take off. There was plenty of paper and fairly dry kindling, so why wasn't it burning better? Within minutes, the entire downstairs was filled with thick white smoke. What the heck was going on?

Gregg and I held a frantic whispered conversation with each other while the smoke continued to billow out of the stove.

"What's going on here, Gregg? Why is it smoking like this?"

"I don't know. Who do you think I am, Daniel Boone?" he asked, laughing at his own response.

I wasn't sure if we should add more paper or find a water bucket and put the whole thing out, when I heard feet hit the floor upstairs. Seconds later, a figure clad in a bathrobe appeared through the haze. It was Marianne, an attractive single mother of two boys who had a no nonsense attitude and a strong backwoods Southern accent. Her brows were knit into a frown, and she gave us a look that made me want to hide.

"What's going on down here?" she whispered. Without waiting for an answer, she reached for the damper on the stovepipe and opened it, giving the fire the draft it needed.

"Now open that there door, and let some of this smoke out of here," she commanded. "We're about to choke to

Chapter Four

death upstairs." I thought I heard her mumble something like, "Don't even know how to build a fire," under her breath as she climbed back up the steps. I was so embarrassed! What a night it had been – and we still had six more to go.

Chapter Five

Money was always an issue on the farm, at least for me. Some people had sold houses or property before they moved to Alaska, and almost everyone sold their cars after they were here for a while. There was no place to drive on the farm and darn few places in Hoonah.

If a person living at Mt. Bether obtained work in town, they were expected to give half of their income, but the money that people received from the sale of houses or cars remained their own.

Though Mt. Bether was a Christian community, there were still classes of people, like anywhere else in the world. No doubt there are those who would vehemently deny that it was so, however, a few days on the farm would reveal that there were the haves and the have-nots. I'm certain that if a dire need came up that couldn't be met any other way, an individual could get help, but for the most part, if something happened like a medical need, you were expected to get a job in town to pay the bill.

As I had mentioned before, we'd spent almost every cent we had just getting to Alaska, so there wasn't much to spare for any frivolous items. We had money enough to buy toothpaste and soap and powdered milk, things of that nature, but that was about it.

Anyway, as I was saying, when it came to money, I didn't have much, so I was delighted when John Borelli approached me one day about working in town. It was only a temporary one-night thing. The barge that supplied Hoonah with almost all of its groceries was arriving that night, and they needed longshoremen to help unload it. I had no idea what the duties entailed, but they were paying five bucks an hour, and it would get me off the farm for a while.

By mid-afternoon, we were on our way to town, having

Chapter Five

gone through the whole fiasco of crossing the mudflats and packing the canoe down to the water. If I recall, there may have been two or three other guys that came to town with me. Most of the single guys were in the same position as me financially, so if there was any work, they jumped at the chance to make a few bucks.

We pulled into the cold storage dock and tied up alongside one of the many trollers that were moored there.

The float was a forest of wooden masts and trolling poles that jutted into the sky. On the city float, some 30 feet away, the much larger seine boats were tied to each other three or four deep. On the opposite side of the float, across from the seine boats, dozens of skiffs were tied up. The water here was much shallower, and on the minus tides, when the water was lower than normal, the skiffs were left high and dry.

As I stepped on the float, I peered over the side to see if there were any fish. What I saw was an underwater junkyard. Amongst the bottles and cans that littered the bottom were old engine blocks, pistons, gaskets, tires and even a few bicycle wheels. Though it was unsightly, it provided a safe haven for a multitude of small fish and eels and an anchor for the orange and white sea anemones that clung to the debris.

On the nearby pilings, clusters of blue-black mussels hung like figs, waiting for the tide to return. Starfish inched ever so slowly across the seabed, and from above, I could make out a Dungeness crab as it made a rapid retreat in reverse toward the eelgrass. It was like gazing into a massive outdoor aquarium.

As luck would have it, the tide was low, leaving the ramp that connected the float to the dock at a steep incline. We fought our way to the top, hanging on to the rotting wooden railing and sidestepping the more obvious weak spots in the gangplank.

"Man, I wish they'd replace this blasted thing," I said to

Wilderness Blues

no one in particular. Going up the ramp was bad enough, but walking down it at low tide really took an act of faith, especially if you were trying to pack something back to the boat, which was almost always the case. Everything from 50-pound boxes of nails to bottles of propane crossed the docks to the boats bound for the farm.

As a group, we worked our way through the muddy streets and up to the town house. As we went, I noticed several small groups of locals looking our way and laughing. They seemed to laugh a lot, and I was left wondering if we were the source of entertainment or if they found everything humorous. One thing was certain, I sure hadn't found too much to laugh about since my arrival at Mt. Bether.

As we walked, I realized that though I knew my fellow travelers by name, there was little else that I knew about them. Aside from living on the farm together, we had very little in common. Not only did I not know these people, most of them I didn't really like. It's not that I especially disliked them, it's just that aside from religion, which I was increasingly unhappy with, we shared no common ground. We weren't friends. There was no getting together after work to discuss the day or planning a fishing trip together. They weren't someone who would come to dinner at my house or enjoy a night of cards. (How carnal!) How could I be living with such a large group of people and still feel so lonely? I pondered these things as we strolled through town.

Reaching the town house, we stripped off our rubber boots and raingear and left them on the front porch. Stepping inside, I was a little disappointed to see that nothing in the house had changed; I was greeted by the same drab walls and furnishings. There was, however, a different woman taking over the chore of housemother.

Housemother was the term given to the lady who took care of the cooking and cleaning at the Mt. Bether town house. She answered the phone and passed messages via the

Chapter Five

radio to the farm. On occasion, she would have to meet the ferry to pick up passengers and freight. She would feed them and house them until they could catch the next boat out. There were times when whole groups of people would show up simultaneously, like a school of salmon at spawning time; some were waiting for the next ferry to Juneau, and some were there to make phone calls or take care of personal business. It would be chaos, but the housemother had to take it all in stride, figuring out meals and sleeping arrangements for everyone. Usually, like the night watch chore, housemother duty lasted a week. As far as I know, most of the ladies enjoyed it; there was shopping, indoor plumbing and a telephone, as well as electric lights, hot water and a real bathtub. I don't believe any of the younger single gals ever got a chance to do it; only the married women or the older widows, someone that had run a house before and had a little experience.

After supper, my fellow longshoremen and I went down to Hoonah Seafoods to await the arrival of the *Klehowa*. That was the name of the tug that towed the barge that serviced many of the smaller outlying towns in Southeast. It usually arrived about once every three weeks and was the topic of many a conversation around town.

"When's the *Klehowa* coming in?"

"They're supposed to be in tonight."

"I hope so. They're out of Ranier at the liquor store."

"Bummer, man, all three stores are out of Sailor Boy crackers, too. I sure hope they aren't late."

Indeed. Being on time was the exception, not the rule. Even though there was a schedule posted with arrival dates, it wasn't always adhered to. For one reason or another, the barge seldom showed when it was expected. Due to bad weather, poor planning or some other unexpected delay, it wasn't unusual for the barge to arrive hours or even days late. That could present some real problems. The barge sup-

Wilderness Blues

plied Hoonah with the vast majority of its groceries and almost everything else necessary to run a town. From bread to meat, cereal to soda pop, it was the least expensive way to receive freight from the lower 48.

The day after it arrived, there would be lots of groceries on the shelves, and business would be brisk. The aisles of the stores were packed with shoppers restocking their pantries. By the second week, there was noticeably less merchandise available. By week three, the store shelves resembled Mother Hubbard's cupboard. If you were able to find what you wanted in any of the three stores, it was probably because no one else wanted it. Large gaps appeared in the shelving, and only the less desirable items were left. There were lots of dusty boxes of pistachio pudding cluttering the space and things like canned garbanzo beans or stewed prunes, but the more popular items like rice or pilot bread were long gone. I'm sure that many a menu revolved around what was available at the local grocers.

There were problems even when the barge did show up on time. Almost anyone in town could tell a story of some mishap involving freight on the *Klehowa* ... household belongings delivered to the wrong port, an entire shipment of fresh eggs stored in one of the onboard freezers, full pallets of soda pop punctured by a careless forklift operator, the list goes on and on. One person watched from the dock as the new fiberglass cruiser he'd ordered slipped from the slings of the barge's crane as the longshoremen and barge employees looked on helplessly. It bounced and slid, screeching across the concrete dock, eventually coming to rest on its side. There was an uncomfortable silence and much shifting of weight from one foot to the next, when finally the vessel's owner stepped forward and, addressing the barge crew, simply stated, "You just bought yourself a boat." Turning around, he walked down to his truck and left. Sometime later, he was the proud owner of a new cruiser, which I

Chapter Five

thought was nicer than the first one anyway. I'm fairly certain he didn't ship this one up on the *Klehowa*.

While we waited for the barge to arrive, my fellow farmers and I took a walk down to the ferry terminal and back. When we returned, I noticed a young native couple sitting on the bull rail at Hoonah Seafoods. They had apparently just come from the bar next door. Glaring at us, the lady screamed, "White honkeys!"

Now, normally such an unprovoked and unexpected outburst would have unnerved me totally, but for some unknown reason, I started to laugh. The man with her swore and slapped her so hard she fell over. Uncertain of what to do in that situation, we all walked off. Of this much I was sure – I didn't want to have the spit slapped out of my mouth.

We returned later as the tug was pulling up to the dock. The native couple had left, for which I was grateful. Strolling down the breezeway to the staging area where the goods were to be unloaded, I could sense the excitement in the air. Forklifts were gassed up, and men were scurrying back and forth, making last minute preparations.

Glancing down over the side of the pier, I could see the longshoremen on the barge poised to lob their lines to the men on the dock. Clouds of white smoke gushed from the stacks of the tug, and the pungent smell of diesel exhaust filled the air as the captain maneuvered closer to the pier. I felt a thud that shook the dock clear down to the street. The pilings groaned in protest as they fought to remain still. For just a moment, I wasn't sure that they'd hold, but they did. Looking around, I could see that no one else seemed the least bit concerned with all the noise and the shaking, so I took some comfort in that.

Within minutes, the first load was lifted to the top of the dock, and we were sent to the store to haul the freight inside. Back and forth the whole night long, from the front of

Wilderness Blues

the store to the stock room, we hand carried every piece. As we entered the backroom, we called out what we had in our hands, and one of the store employees directed us to the proper area.

"Best Foods Mayonnaise!"

"Aisle three."

"Sailor Boy Pilot Bread?"

"Top shelf on your left."

"Where do you want the Hunts tomato sauce?"

"Put it next to the canned corn on aisle two, near the middle."

We rushed back and forth, bumping into each other in the narrow aisles.

The storage area went from practically bare to overflowing. When we ran out of room on the shelves, we put stuff on the floor. It was amazing to see the transformation from empty to full, and it was fun to be a part of it. When all the dry goods were put away, we moved across the street and proceeded to fill the freezers with meat and bread, pastries and ice cream.

Finishing that chore, we worked our way back to the dock. The loading platform was piled with 100-pound bottles of propane and cribs filled with hardware. There were couches and chairs, stacks of roofing and plywood and pallet after pallet of heavy cardboard totes used for shipping frozen fish, bound for the cold storage. This barge was truly a lifeline to the outside world. Sometime during the wee hours of the morning, our task was completed, and the barge was untied. The deep throaty blast of the tug's horn shattered the stillness of the night and echoed down the bay, passing from mountain to mountain. They were off to the next port.

"Man, I wish the bar was still open," one local commented, as we all started to leave.

"It wouldn't do you any good, anyway," came the reply.

Chapter Five

"We don't get paid till tomorrow."

"Oh." He shrugged. "I guess I'll see ya then, partner."

It had been a long night, and I was tired but happy. I'd made enough money to buy some toothpaste and a few snacks to take home to Jan and the kids. In the morning, we'd catch the boat back out to the farm, and it would be business as usual. The very thought caused my spirit to sink. The idea of returning to the farm was almost more than I could stand. More than once, I entertained the idea of just taking off, but that wasn't even an option. My family was still there, and there was no way I was going to leave them.

Chapter Six

By the beginning of September, there was a notable change in the weather. The long days of summer had peaked and were rapidly winding down. By month's end, we would lose about two hours of daylight. The summer's heat, much like the light, was dwindling, and on several mornings, I saw my breath, much to my dismay.

The rain began to fall more frequently (something I didn't think was possible) and with more intensity. It was cold and was often driven by chilly winds that forced it into any open collar, where it would drip down your back in painfully frigid drops and soak your clothes.

In the fields, the last of the fireweed had bloomed, its magenta blossoms shriveling and turning white with next year's seed.

The cottonwoods that grew on Game Point had already started the transition to gold so that they stood out boldly against the monochromatic greens of the forest behind them, and the muskegs that bordered the camp were changing from the cheery living shades of emerald, lime and olive to a more somber yellow and brown.

The steady downpours turned the clean, clear water of Game Creek into a dark, rumbling river, which eroded the banks and pulled trees into its depths as it rushed to the bay, scouring the bottom as it went.

Day after day, I awoke to the drumming of rain on the roof.

"Man, I hate this place," I said softly, looking out at the gloom.

I felt compelled to remind God that he'd promised that he wouldn't destroy the earth by water again. As I recall, we had precipitation in one form or another for 39 days

Chapter Six

straight. I considered changing my name to Noah and getting in the boat building business.

The many days of cold rain had left water standing in the fields, turning them into muddy quagmires.

The muck was sticky and clung to our boots, making every step a challenge. As soon as we entered the fields, our boots became caked with sticky, heavy, brown mud. It clung to our neoprenes like burrs on a dog. Our feet seemed anchored to the ground by the weight, so forward motion was a struggle. By day's end, we were drained just from the effort of walking.

Nonetheless, it was time to harvest the limited variety of crops that would grow here. Frankly, it surprised me that anything could grow here at all, it was so wet. As it was though, the long summer days seemed to provide a few hardy vegetables with what they needed in the way of nutrition. The fact that they didn't drown seemed like a miracle. Incredibly, many of the root crops seemed to do quite well, especially carrots, beets, turnips and potatoes. Members of the cabbage family did favorably, too, with some of the cabbages getting well over 20 pounds. Of course, zucchini squash also prospered, which, I guess, was no big surprise. Apparently, they are prolific, kind of like the rabbits of the vegetable world.

Unfortunately for me, there was another root vegetable that seemed to enjoy the environment here. It was the rutabaga. Even its name sounded nasty, kind of like something you might find on your skin that would require a doctor's care. Shaped like a turnip, the top third was a dull purple color, with the remainder a putrid yellow-brown. Long, thread-like roots grew all around the bottom of the plant, giving it the appearance of growing a thin, wispy beard. Rock hard and woody in texture, they didn't lend themselves to being eaten raw. Even the root maggots that attacked the tuber could leave only the shallowest of canals as they ate

Wilderness Blues

their way across the tough surface.

Prior to coming to Alaska, I had never even heard of a rutabaga before. I guess I'd lived a pretty sheltered life. In my several years of working in supermarkets from Ohio to Key West, I had never been exposed to one. If they were hanging out in the produce section somewhere, the manager apparently had them hidden. He was probably too embarrassed to display them with the fruits and vegetables that most normal folks would purchase. Perhaps they were only available by special request. I can see it all now; a shady character would approach the stockroom doors in the rear of the store and have a whispered conversation with the produce clerk. The clerk would disappear for a few seconds, and when he came back, would hand off a brown paper bag to the man. There would be an exchange of money, and the man would hurry off, glancing nervously as he slinked out of the store. Well, maybe they weren't quite that bad, but if ever there were a sinister vegetable, it would be the rutabaga.

Like many of the other misconceptions I'd had prior to coming to the farm, harvesting the crops was not what I had expected. For some unknown reason, I was still embracing schoolboy thoughts of sheaves of corn stalks and pumpkins languishing about in fields. The few months that I had been on the farm should have extinguished any such foolish, childish, romantic thoughts. The reality of harvest was, at least for us, far different.

Though there was no shortage of misery to go around, there were still some pleasant distractions that only Alaska could offer. Strings of sand hill cranes flew high overhead daily, wave after wave announcing their arrival with high-pitched squawking that could be heard long before they came into view. From our vantage point in the fields, we craned our necks, watching as each string dissolved when they approached Ear Mountain. Circling and circling, they climbed higher and higher, catching the updraft until they

Chapter Six

conquered the summit and reassembled on the other side to continue their journey south.

Each evening, as twilight was settling over the land, the silence was broken by the piercing honks of Canada Geese, as they searched the marshy fields and mudflats for a place to spend the night. Green wing teals rocketed past our heads in a zigzag pattern, and mallards found protection in the calm waters of the brackish sloughs that cut through the fields. Periodically, the reports of shotgun blasts echoed from across the bay, as waterfowl hunters took advantage of the abundance of birds.

Occasionally, in the fields further from camp, we would spot deer feeding on the sweet pea vines. My first inclination was to grab a gun and shoot them. We desperately needed the meat, but the powers that be wouldn't permit it – too close to camp I guess, so we just chased them off.

More than a few times on our way out to the potato fields, we came across bear crap on the road. This wasn't so unusual since the valley was a natural gathering place for brown bears. What caught my eye about these particular piles of poop was what was in them. I don't make a habit of checking out animal droppings (though I understand some very good hunters do). What made these droppings so interesting was that they were full of carrots! Some brownie had plowed up several rows with his paw and had a feast; I wished they were as fond of rutabagas. I could see if we were going to make it through the winter, we'd have to harvest the crops before the wild animals did. Our very lives were dependent on the food we could gather from the fields, so with the exception of the very old or very young, everyone was expected to gather in the gardens and do their part.

Once we were in the fields, everyone picked a tool of some sort, depending on what we were to harvest that day. If it were cabbages, carrots, turnips or rutabagas, a knife to

Wilderness Blues

trim the greens or sever the plant would do. For potatoes, a pitchfork seemed to work best, but there was never enough to go around, so we used whatever was available; hoes, clam rakes, shovels, anything to turn over the mud and expose the tubers. A good many potatoes were chopped or run through. If they were caught in time, they could be eaten right away, but there were so many damaged that quite a few were just fed to the pigs.

Because it was considered a "family project," even the kids were out in the fields. They were given the job of picking up the spuds and putting them in the buckets, where they were then transported to a wagon and taken back to the tabernacle to dry.

Located inside the tabernacle were a dozen or so drying racks made just for the potatoes. They were simple: chicken wire stretched over some one-by-six boards. About as large as a sheet of plywood, they were made to stack one upon another with airspace between to allow the heat to circulate. The racks were a necessary part of the harvest; the spuds arrived from the fields wet and caked with mud and would rot if they were stored in the root cellar that way.

As it was, a lot of them spoiled anyway, so every few weeks or so, we had to light our gas lanterns and reluctantly crawl into the cellar and sort.

Dressed in raingear and carrying empty buckets, two or three of us would walk into the root cellar. Though the sawdust in the walls was 12 inches thick, it was still cold in there and dark as Hades. There were no windows in the building, and the dark wooden walls seemed to absorb the light from our lanterns like a sponge absorbs water. The air was heavy with the smells of dirt and sawdust and rotting vegetables. Down the narrow aisle we bumped along, stopping at the bins piled high with potatoes. Crawling onto them, we started sorting. Whether you sat, lay or kneeled, there was no comfortable position to be found. The lumpy tubers

Chapter Six

poked at our bodies, leaving them cold and aching. We sat on the shifting piles, flinging the good ones into empty bins, the bad into the buckets. In the dim light, you wouldn't know if what you grabbed was spoiled or not, until your fingers plunged through it. The stench is impossible to describe. Let it suffice to say that the smell of rotten potatoes could literally make one gag.

Back in the tabernacle, all the mud that had come in on the potatoes was now resting on the wooden floor. During the process of drying, the spuds had to be turned so they would dry evenly, which meant clumps of dry mud ended up under the racks. Of course, it had to be swept up when the racks were empty, so clouds of dust settled on everything. For weeks after harvest, the dust crept up out of the cracks in the floor and coated every surface in the building. It even managed to work its way into the apartments upstairs.

One of the more pleasant things we did in the fall was to prepare the cabbage for sauerkraut. The work wasn't hard – just cut the heads of cabbage into thin strips, stuff it in a barrel and cover the whole mess with salt. A wooden lid was placed over it with a rock on top, and the fermenting process started. For some reason, I got considerable satisfaction working on it. In a few evenings' time, we'd made all the sauerkraut that we could possibly eat in a year. Though my part in the process was minimal, I felt good about having a hand in processing food for the winter. Fortunately for me, I happened to like sauerkraut, which was good, since we ate it at least once a week, much to the displeasure of several of the other members.

By the end of October, all the fields were harvested. Some of the vegetables were canned, the rest were stored in the root cellar or dried, with the exception of the sauerkraut. It was time to hunker down and get ready for winter, something I wasn't looking forward to. I hoped we had enough food.

Chapter Seven

By November of 1976, most of the work on the tabernacle had been completed.

It was a monster of a building, maybe 75 feet or so long and at least 30 feet wide. I can't really remember the exact dimensions. It was two stories high with an attic above the upper floor. Until the barn was built several years later, it was by far the largest building in the camp and was easily seen by boats passing by out in the bay, a mile or so away.

The downstairs served as the meeting area where church was held. As part of the corporate life mentality, the eldership decided to turn part of the building into a dining hall, so we could eat all of our meals together. Tables and benches were constructed, and the whole dining area looked like one giant picnic was going to take place.

A kitchen was built in the far end of the tabernacle that took up almost a third of the space. It had hundreds of square feet of shelf space and dozens of cupboards, though there was little food to store in them. Linoleum had been laid on the kitchen floor for sanitary reasons, I guess, which gave it a finished look that most of the other buildings lacked. The enormous wood cook stove was moved there, and during the day, it helped to heat the apartments upstairs.

Some benches were slapped together for the meeting hall, also, and like the ones in the dining area, they had no backrests or cushions. I'm not sure why, maybe it was part of the death to self way of life. In any event, they weren't very comfortable. They were built with green, rough-cut lumber, and I was always a little afraid that the kids might slide across one of the seats and pick up a splinter, but to the best of my knowledge that never happened. By the time we left 10 years later, those benches were as smooth as if

Wilderness Blues

they'd been run through a planer; however, our butts may have been a little calloused.

Work on the tabernacle had been completed none too soon. A fire destroyed one of the cabins that housed four families. (All of the cabins had multiple families living in them, at least for the first year or two.) In fact, I was upstairs counseling with Barbara Boryslaw, one of the elders, when it happened.

Barbara was a bit of a study in contrasts. Prematurely gray in her mid-30s, she still had bouts of acne, which became more pronounced when she was preaching. Though she was as big as a house with child number six, she had a matronly air about her as she dispensed spiritual wisdom, like a saintly gumball machine. She had a rather dry sense of humor that seemed to evaporate during church services, which she took very seriously. When it was time for a meeting, she frequently grabbed a tambourine, which she shook violently as she led the congregation in song.

During the counseling session, I was lamenting the fact that the farm didn't even celebrate Christmas (or any other holiday for that matter), when we heard Denise Brown anxiously calling outside the window. Petite and attractive, with dark brown wavy hair, she was the mother of three young boys who, along with her husband, occupied a room in the cabin next door.

"Sister Barbara! Sister Barbara!" she shouted.

"Yes, Denise?" she replied. Barbara had the kind of voice that made you believe that everything was under control. She was always cool, calm and collected unless she was delivering the word—then she was almost fanatical.

"FIRE!" Denise exclaimed.

"Where?" Barbara asked calmly.

"In your house!" came the reply.

Needless to say, the counseling session was over. Word spread through the camp quickly, and everyone came out to

Chapter Seven

help. For the first 20 minutes or so, the fire was confined to one of the upstairs rooms where it had started. People were rushing in and out of the downstairs, snatching anything that they could get their hands on, passing it through the door and tossing it out the windows. Clothing, curtains, mattresses, guns, it didn't matter; we were in a race against time. I helped someone lift a bed in Bill and Sandy's room and there, underneath, was a whole case of Milky Way candy bars. Believe me, if my hands hadn't been full of bed, I'd have damn sure grabbed that candy. As it was, on the next trip back into the blaze, the Milky Ways were gone. I just assumed that Uncle Bill scarfed them up. I was hoping he might pass them out as a way of thanksgiving for salvaging his stuff, but no such luck. Bill was pretty fond of his sweets. For the remainder of the day, my mind returned to the sight of that case of candy bars and the opportunity lost. It wasn't until some years later, when Bill and I were reminiscing, that he said it wasn't him that took that candy. Guess we'll never know who did.

As luck would have it, the tide was high, so every five-gallon bucket in camp was pressed into service for a bucket brigade that stretched from the mudflats to the inferno in front of us. The heat was so intense that the little bit of water that we were able to toss on it just hissed and evaporated in a puff of steam. Flames shot through the windows and raced unchecked up to the roof. The bone-dry wood snapped and popped as it yielded to the fire, and somewhere inside, the heat ignited a box of bullets that went off sporadically.

By nightfall, all that remained of the cabin was a square-shaped mound of red-orange coals. A few of us volunteered to watch the embers, to make sure the wind didn't spread them. Someone brought us over some potatoes to bake in the ashes. It was a nice gesture, but without butter or salt they were a little bland – and they sure weren't Milky Ways.

Wilderness Blues

After the fire, the whole upstairs of the tabernacle was turned into living quarters to accommodate all the people that had been displaced. It was sectioned off into 12 x 15 foot rooms, and a person received one or two rooms, depending on the size of the family he had.

By early November, Jan, the girls and I joined the refugees in the tabernacle. It had become apparent that we couldn't spend the winter in that travel trailer; it was just too cold, and the propane for the heater was too expensive.

We were assigned to one of the rooms upstairs. They were painfully small, so each family had to do the best they could to make their space a home. It was challenging to find the most efficient use of the limited space available.

We built a closet along one wall that separated the girls' sleeping area from ours. With lumber from the mill, we put together a double bed and topped it with a couple of twin-size, four-inch foam mattresses from Sears. All things considered, it was fairly comfortable. I made a small washstand from one-by-eight boards. It had a shelf for storing the dishpan we used for washing up and a curtain to hide the porta-potty that was stored underneath. With the closet and the few pieces of furniture in the room, there was just enough space to walk around the bed. A set of bunk beds and a children's table and chair set pretty well took up the area in the girls' room.

The outside walls and ceilings of the rooms were finished in sheetrock, with the interior walls comprised of spruce or hemlock boards nailed vertically in place. As the green wood dried out, it shrank and split, making privacy an issue.

Each room had a skylight made of corrugated plastic roofing that yellowed with time. There was also a small window in the room that provided some light. The girls' room was dark and dismal, almost dungeon-like on all but the sunniest of days, which were few and far between. I felt awful

Chapter Seven

that my children's space was so drab, but it was all we had, and they didn't seem to mind.

The door of our room opened out into a narrow, dimly lit hallway, which was adorned with an assortment of coats, hats, scarves, boots and raingear up and down its entire length. At times, walking down that dark hallway was like passing through a gauntlet, tripping over boots and knocking down coats on our way to or from the apartment. This was especially challenging when it was time to take the porta-potty to the outhouse. (Every household had a porta-potty, slop jar, honey bucket, whatever you want to call it, for nighttime use.) With a flashlight in one hand and the potty in the other, you would have to weave your way around the clothes and other clutter that littered the corridor. Occasionally, someone would send their kids to do the dirty deed and the next morning, the overpowering smell of Pine Sol would permeate the hallway, evidence of a spill.

Though the stove downstairs consumed massive amounts of wood, it wasn't sufficient to provide enough heat to the upstairs apartments. Since there were no vents between floors, most of the residents had to purchase some form of supplemental heat, which in our case was an Alladin kerosene heater. It was round, green and stood about two feet tall on four short legs. It was about 12 inches in diameter, which meant a teakettle fit quite nicely on it. All things considered, the Aladdin heated the rooms fairly well, but if the wick wasn't trimmed correctly, it left an overpowering stench of diesel fumes. After being in a room with the Alladin for a few minutes, my eyes would start to burn and water. The only recourse was to open the window and let some fresh air in, which of course cooled down the room. It seemed like everything on the farm was an endless cycle of choices. You could accept something bad or choose something worse.

Privacy was certainly an issue for all the residents of the

Wilderness Blues

tabernacle apartments. Our apartment, if that was what you wanted to call it, was located in the middle of the building, with rooms on both sides. With few exceptions, an inch of spruce or hemlock was all that separated the rooms. It was basically the same arrangement as the outhouses where sound passed back and forth so freely. Two young, single gals were our neighbors, and it wasn't uncommon to carry on a conversation with them through the walls in the evening. There were a few times when paper, snacks or reading material were passed between the rooms without ever opening a door. Of course, arguments, passion or even lifting the lid on the potty could be readily heard. A walk down the hallway at night was a revealing peek into the residents' lives.

The room on the other side of us was considered a sewing room for Amanda's youngest daughter. On more than a few evenings, several young people would gather there and socialize. It usually started off with just talking, but eventually, someone would pick up a guitar and a little sing along would start in, and before I knew it, I was subjected to an unwanted serenade. Of course, there was no way to say anything without looking like a complete jerk, so I usually stewed for a while before I got angry enough to go next door and ask them to hold it down.

The floor didn't provide much soundproofing, either. Most nights we could hear the sounds of the night watch as he walked around downstairs, his gas lantern hissing, and the heavy tabernacle door closing with a whooshing sound as he left on his appointed rounds. I didn't realize that sound traveled just as well from the top down until one morning, a friend who had been on night watch came and thanked me for the previous night's entertainment. I had been telling Jan about an act I had seen on one of the late night talk shows where a guy placed his hand under his armpit and played "Sweet Georgia Brown," and I proceeded to imitate the farting sounds. I had no idea that I had an un-

Chapter Seven

seen audience and thereafter resolved to be more aware of the noise that came from our place.

Living accommodations throughout the farm were shaky at best those first few years. Though we didn't have to live in Army tents like the first settlers here did, and we were no longer confined to a damp trailer, there were still a lot of trials. The tabernacle was the focal point of the farm, and since all the meetings, Bible studies and dining took place there, it was the noisiest building in camp.

Without fail, we would be awakened before five each morning as the night watch chopped kindling downstairs in the kitchen, each blow from the ax echoing in the large, empty room. For the life of me, I don't know why the kindling wasn't chopped the night before, but it never was. Of course, the noise woke not only me but the girls as well, who, once awakened, didn't see the need to go back to sleep. Several years later when the farm acquired some cows, the milking crew started even earlier. Shuffling feet and clanging the stainless milk buckets, the men would prepare to head to the barn, oblivious to the racket that was telegraphed through the floor. I mentioned the noise several times when we all gathered for a meal, but my complaints seemed to fall on deaf ears. Most days, I just lay in bed and waited for the folks downstairs to leave so I could catch a few more minutes of sleep. It was just one more thing to deal with. It was frustrating to be so powerless, so unable to change the situation.

There was a kind of double standard concerning noise in the tabernacle. Apparently, it was okay to flow from the bottom up, but it was considered distracting or disruptive to flow from the top down. Those of us living upstairs were supposed to keep it down so as not to disturb any activities that may be going on down below. One night, Barbara Boryslaw came to the door, complaining that my girls were dropping crayons through the knothole in the floor. Appar-

Wilderness Blues

ently, they were landing on one of the tables and disturbing the Bible study she was trying to conduct. She wanted Jan to keep the girls quiet and stop the mischief. I don't recall exactly what Jan said, but it was something to the effect that if Barbara wanted to have a Bible study, she should do it in her house, because she wasn't going to keep our daughters from playing in their own home.

When I heard about the incident, I was delighted that Jan had stood her ground. So often we had both endured or just accepted what the eldership said to do. Though it was a small thing, I felt like I had gained an important ally. However, it was to be a long time before she started to share my mindset concerning most of what went on at the farm.

We lived in the tabernacle for about five years – five very long years. We moved from that first small apartment as our family grew and as larger apartments became available. More people were building their own cabins, thus freeing up additional space. Though we were always a little cramped and the noise was a continual issue, I was reluctant to build a cabin for us. It would be like putting down permanent roots, which I most definitely didn't want to do.

Chapter Eight

December arrived cold and blustery, the dark gray clouds dumping snow one day and rain the next, turning the roads around the camp into a muddy quagmire that bogged down the tractor and tried the strength of the animals and the resolve of the men.

The daily chore of chopping firewood was made more difficult by the slush that covered every stick of wood.

Wool or cotton gloves were almost useless for most of the outdoor work; within minutes, the moisture saturated the material, and your hands would ache from the cold. Those who could afford to purchase a pair of Fireball gloves were the envy of the camp, though the stiff, thick fingers gave you the appearance of having Mickey Mouse hands. Coated with fluorescent orange neoprene, they offered some protection from the wet and cold, though it was short-lived. The material didn't breathe, so after a day or two, perspiration dampened the insulation inside so your hands still got cold. It was another no win situation.

While the rest of the country was in a holiday mood, things on the farm were as bland and depressing as usual. Thanksgiving had come and gone without so much as an acknowledgement of the day. There were no turkey dinners or family gatherings, certainly no football games or parades on television. If I hadn't glanced at a calendar, I'd never have known that the holidays were upon us. There wasn't a strand of tinsel or a string of lights to be seen anywhere in the camp; in all my days, I'd never seen such a somber place. Even worse, I saw no end in sight. Stretching off into the distance, as far as I could see, one dreadful day would lead to the next. Whatever the goal was, whatever the vision that kept people here, I didn't share it. Maybe I was too carnal, too willing to gratify the flesh man

Wilderness Blues

(I'd heard that a few times), I don't know. I didn't want to walk in the spirit or move on to perfection; I just wanted to be me. I just wanted to be happy. That didn't seem like such a bad thing.

There was a saying on the farm. Actually, there were quite a few sayings on the farm. Anyway, whenever anyone was having a hard time they were said to be "going through the fire." As much as I *went through the fire* on the farm, it's a wonder I wasn't reduced to a cinder.

Shortly after Thanksgiving, I decided to take a trip south to see my folks. We had some cash because I had sold our car after discovering that the windshield wiper was missing. The car had been parked at the city warehouse unattended and was fair game for thieves. Fearing that parts would gradually disappear with it in town and me at the farm, I decided to sell it. Cars weren't very common in Hoonah at the time and were somewhat of a status symbol. I had no problem selling it for a fair price, though I had to think long and hard about actually letting it go. After all, it was our way out of here. Selling it meant that I was going to be stuck here. However, we needed the money for our everyday expenses and the occasional trip to town for snacks, so I opted for the short-term gratification of immediate cash.

The decision to leave came one night as I was sitting alone in my room. Jan and the girls had already left for the church meeting, and I was upstairs getting cleaned up. The foul, gloomy weather, the separation from my family and friends, the lack of everyday comforts and the overwhelming feelings of loneliness seemed to come to a head that night. To make matters worse, Jan seemed to be adapting to the lifestyle just fine. She didn't share my sense of anger or despair and didn't want to hear my complaints anymore. I was feeling isolated from the person I most loved, and I felt like the farm was to blame.

Sitting on my bed, the sinister clouds of depression that

Chapter Eight

had dogged me since my first day there finally bore fruit. Alone in the darkness of my room, I started to weep. All the frustration and anger and feelings of hopelessness came pouring out. I felt like an orphan, abandoned by God in this location where God was all people talked about. If he was really here, why did I feel this way? Confused and angry with myself for being so weak, I vowed to never let myself get so low again. I was going to take control of whatever circumstances that I could in my life, and my first priority was leaving this place. I needed some time to myself to try and sort out what was going on, and I sure wasn't going to get it here. The very thought of getting off the farm left me feeling giddy. In one 10-minute block of time, I went from despair to euphoria. There was no doubt about it — this place was driving me nuts!

With the feeling of power that my decision had given me, I announced the next day that I needed to go to town to make arrangements for a trip. I would be leaving the farm for an undetermined amount of time. I don't really recall, but I'm sure that the eldership wanted to seek visions to see if it was God's will for me to leave. But at that point, I couldn't have cared less. I was leaving one way or another, and if they didn't like it, they could stuff it up wherever!

The day of my departure was somewhat bittersweet. I dearly loved my wife and kids, but I had to get off that farm. Frankly, I felt sure that I would never see my family again. I was fully convinced that God was going to punish me for leaving, and I would surely be the cause of an airplane accident. I felt really bad for the innocent lives that would be lost because of my act of rebellion, but at that point, I didn't really care. I knew I was going to be cast into hell for my selfish act, but I thought, "Thunderation! Can hell be any worse than living here?"

Jan confided at a later date that she wasn't sure that I would be coming back, though not for the same paranoid

Wilderness Blues

reasons that I had. She knew that I was miserable, and she wasn't sure if she and the girls would be enough of an incentive for me to return.

As it turned out, I wasn't the only one to run away from the farm. My good friend, Uncle Bill, had left several times, and I'm quite certain he would have stayed in the lower 48 if his family wasn't back at the camp. There were several other folks that left to preserve their sanity as well, though I can't place their names at the moment. One person that does come to mind though is Jeri T., the big gal that unintentionally shot the full moon at the outhouse. Though there was never any outward appearance to suggest that she was ever anything but a jolly soul, Jeri was struggling like everyone else. She was single, broke and doing whatever menial job she was assigned to each day. One day, she appeared before the elders saying that her mother was dreadfully ill, and she needed to get home. She had no funds, and there was no time for her to find a job, so the farm paid her way. As it turned out, a few weeks later, someone heard from her mother. She wasn't sick nor had she been recently. Jeri had made the whole story up in order to get away. Of course, the eldership never bothered to explain why she wasn't coming back. I found out about it via the rumor mill. When I heard the news, I was ecstatic! It was like being detained on Alcatraz and hearing that a fellow inmate had escaped. I certainly wished her well.

There were several small airlines that flew between Juneau and the other small communities in Southeast. It was the only way to leave the island, other than ferry or small boat, and it was by far the quickest.

Catching a flight on one of the local commuter airlines, I arrived in Juneau about 25 minutes later. Walking through the doors of the airport, I was immediately besieged by the sights and sounds and smells all around me. There were people rushing to catch planes, pushing past me in a blur of

Chapter Eight

color, towing suitcases and duffle bags. Off to the side, a pair of crusty looking fellows in baseball caps and worn wool jackets were discussing fish prices. They smelled of diesel fuel and old bait. At the main airline counter stood a man dressed in a suit with a coat draped over one arm and a briefcase in the other. Around the corner, someone had lit a cigarette, and the scent was competing for my attention with the aroma wafting down from the restaurant upstairs. An overhead speaker announced the arrival of some flight, and outside I heard the roar of a single engine plane as it taxied to the runway.

I had a few hours before my flight left, so I decided to get a burger at the airport restaurant. It was heavenly. It had been months since I'd tasted a hamburger, so I savored every juicy bite.

After paying for the meal, I did a mental calculation of how much money I had left. I wanted to make sure I had enough funds to take care of myself when I got back to the folks' house; partly because I didn't want to be a burden to anyone, but also because I wanted to be totally independent. As much as possible, I wanted to be in complete control of my life, something that I had very little of on the farm.

I'd satisfied one desire with the meal I'd just eaten; now I was going to satisfy another.

Within easy walking distance of the airport there was a small supermarket. I knew they had cigarettes there, so I sauntered on over and bought a pack – Larks, the brand I had smoked for years. They had a catchy jingle and an attractive package. My hands shook in anticipation as I tore the pack open. I lit up and was surprised at how easily I adapted to smoking again, though I did have to find a bench to sit on until my head quit spinning.

I returned to the airport and lit up another cigarette. I was feeling apprehensive about the whole trip. Perhaps it was just the excitement of leaving or the hustle and bustle

Wilderness Blues

and noise of the airport. It could have been that I was afraid that someone I knew might see me there smoking and tell the elders about it. I just wanted to get underway and leave this place behind.

I finally boarded the jet and made my way back to Ohio. The trip was uneventful, and my prophecy of death and destruction proved to be wrong, at least on the way south. Maybe God was going to get me on the return trip. I would probably have racked up such an impressive list of sins by then that he would have no choice but to bring the full force of his righteous judgment upon me.

My folks met me at the Columbus airport, and while they were glad to see me, they had lots of questions for which I had no answers. I remembered the admonition from the pulpit to be silent about the activities of the farm. (We were the first fruits, the chosen people of God. How could anyone outside of the Body of Christ possibly understand what we were doing?) Though at the time it seemed like if we were doing something good it should be shared, we were told not to. I remember the alarm bells going off inside my head when I heard that, but the elders were so religious and seemed to know scripture much better than I, so I just didn't say much. What could I say? I didn't know enough about why I was on the farm to satisfy myself, so how could I possibly explain what was going on to anyone else?

"How was the flight, Tom?" my mom asked.

"Good," I said. "Long. I almost missed my plane in Seattle because of snow in Sitka."

"I bet you're tired aren't you, honey?" she asked sympathetically.

"Yeah," I replied, trying to sound as tired as I could without appearing wimpy. I was hoping to avoid the inevitable prying questions that I knew would come.

"How are Jan and the girls doing?" she asked. Before I could reply, she quipped, "Those pictures you sent last

Chapter Eight

month were just darling! That Liz has such curly hair, almost frizzy, and Jennifer with those big brown eyes and that smile, they just look so sweet! I wish you all could have come."

"Yeah, me too, Mom."

"Is Jan doing alright? She looked a little thin in the photographs. Is she trying to lose weight? She didn't look heavy to me when you guys left to go up there. You look like you may have lost a few pounds, too, Tom. Don't you eat well on that farm?"

"Jan's fine," I replied. "We get enough food I suppose, just not a lot of variety, and there is so much physical work that I guess we just burn it all up."

What I really wanted to say was, "Heck no, we're not getting enough food! Could you send up a goody box loaded with brownies and chocolate chip cookies? Shoot, throw in a few cans of Spam and some chili while you're at it. We'll even eat the stuff that's been collecting dust in the back of the cupboards for months. Could you just read between the lines, folks! Send in the cavalry! Can't you see I'm in over my head, and I don't know what to do? I've screwed up big this time, and I'm too embarrassed to ask for help!" But that's not what I said. I made excuses and tried to make everything appear fine, but everyone that saw me knew that things weren't okay.

As he drove, Dad periodically looked in the rearview mirror at me. I could see his dark brown eyes in the reflection as we passed by the lights along the highway.

My dad had a way of asking questions that made you feel like you were talking to God or something. It's like he knew the answer before you responded to the question, so there was no sense in lying because he already knew the truth. He could be very blunt and straightforward, unlike me. I hate confrontation and go to great lengths to avoid it, even compromising what I want to keep the peace.

Wilderness Blues

When he finally spoke, he was frank and to the point.

"Something sounds fishy to me, Tom. What the hell are you guys doing up there? Are you involved in some kind of a cult?"

His questions hit me like a fist to the guts. I had this feeling like I was a little kid again and had to answer for my actions.

"A cult," I stammered. "No, it's just a bunch of people living on a farm trying to be self-sufficient. There is a feeling that God has called us out to the wilderness to be part of a first fruits company."

I mumbled some other things that I had heard from the pulpit. Things that in the company of the other farmers kind of made sense, but sitting in my parents' car just sounded like so much crap.

I didn't bother to tell them that money would be no good, and chaos was soon to be coming upon the world, and only a select few people would be able to escape the coming doom. At least, that's what was preached. I felt foolish enough just saying the little bit that I had.

He spoke again. "Well, I don't know about that damn farm. I don't trust that Amanda. I didn't like her when I met her. She seems kind of sneaky to me." He paused for a minute to see if I would respond, and when I didn't, he continued on. "I sure hope you know what you're doing, Tom. You've got a lot of responsibility with Jan and those two little girls, and I don't want anything happening to them grandbabies of mine!"

"Yeah, I think I know what I'm doing, Dad," I replied weakly, but the reality was, nothing could be further from the truth.

Chapter Nine

My paranoid behavior did little to satisfy my parents' curiosity about Mt. Bether. In an earlier letter, I had written that I had quit smoking; now, here I was, back to the same old nasty habit less than 12 hours after I stepped off the farm. Though I was a grown man with children of my own, I didn't want my folks to find out I was smoking again, so I made up some phony excuse about having to spend the nights at my in-laws' house in town. Jan's father was a heavy smoker, and I knew that the scent of tobacco that would cling to my clothes would go unnoticed in their home.

Every day, I drove the eight miles or so to my folks' house where I spent the day doing odd jobs, and every evening, I went back to spend the night in town. I withdrew into myself, spending a good bit of time alone and tried to avoid contact with other people as much as possible, which was a little difficult. Living in Alaska elevated me to celebrity status with some folks, and they had lots of questions. As much as possible, I gave vague answers about the farm. Without a doubt, my bizarre conduct surely left everyone wondering what was troubling me, and of a certainty, I was questioning my own sanity.

I spent Christmas and New Years in Ohio, but the holidays just weren't the same without Jan and the kids. With no schedule to follow, I had lots of time to think about my situation. The more I thought, the more confused I became. There wasn't anyone I could talk to about what was troubling me, and it left me feeling very isolated. Even my prayers seemed to be going unanswered. At one point, I thought about contacting the FBI, but what would I say to them? "Hi, I live on a farm in Alaska with a bunch of religious people. Will you run a background check on them?" To the best of my knowledge, no one was doing anything

Wilderness Blues

wrong. I was there of my own choosing, even if the logic was flawed.

Sometime after the holidays, I got the unmistakable feeling that I needed to return to Alaska. I missed Jan and the girls, and in the back of my mind, I was a little afraid that if I wasn't around to kind of balance things out, Jan might get totally brainwashed, and we would never be able to leave the farm as a complete family.

I bid my folks farewell at the Columbus airport and caught a flight bound for Seattle. After we arrived, I made the long trek to the Alaska Airlines terminal. Throngs of people went rushing by: important looking men in business attire and ladies in dresses and pants suits, all dolled up with nice hairdos and perfume. I saw more than a few people with shorts and goofy straw hats looking tanned and happy, testimony to a vacation someplace warm.

"Who the heck goes to Alaska in January?" I thought. "People with any common sense go someplace warm for the winter." Guess I was never accused of having an overabundance of common sense.

Entering the Alaska Airlines terminal, I was struck with feelings of both happiness and depression, simultaneously. My time out in the world was rapidly running down. I was really looking forward to being with my wife and children again, but returning to the farm was like hitting myself in the head with a hammer. I knew it was going to hurt. To make matters worse, I would have to quit smoking all over again. In the meantime though, I planned to make the most of my remaining free time. For the next few hours, I intended to enjoy every last cigarette, right down to the filter.

Chapter Ten

I returned to the farm with some apprehension. I didn't really want to come back, but I couldn't very well leave my family behind, so I didn't have much choice but to return.

I caught a ride out in the jitney and braced myself against the cold. The whole area was coated in snow, from the top of the mountains to the beach.

Some folks would say it was beautiful, and I guess it would be if you were in a ski lodge somewhere, sipping hot chocolate by a roaring fire, but I was in an open boat, struggling to stay warm. The countryside was shades of black and white and grey, and the overcast skies were dark and threatening. The bay was the color of pewter with occasional whitecaps churning the surface of the water. It was a typical winter day in Southeast Alaska.

When we rounded the point, I could hear the roar of several chainsaws and could see figures on the beach chopping firewood. The smoke from multiple chimneys rose and collected in a cloud that hovered over the camp like a blanket. Not much had changed in the time I had been gone; it was the same old stuff, just a different day.

Unfortunately, I came back with the same sour attitude that I'd departed with, and perhaps, if anything, it was worse. My trip to the land of the free left me feeling less willing to blindly submit to the eldership. At one point, I composed a letter to the elders, more or less spelling out my feelings, along with a timeline of how long I would remain on the farm. I wanted to feel like I had some control over my miserable life. I knew that the eldership met every Tuesday afternoon, so one day, after I had been back for about a week, I decided to deliver the letter to them. They were meeting in Sandy's room just down the hall.

Wilderness Blues

Standing nervously outside the door, I knocked. I could hear muffled voices and laughter through the walls. I had expected Sandy to answer, so it was a most unpleasant surprise when Larry Boryslaw came to the door instead. He was the same guy that rambled off that list of do's and don'ts when we first arrived. Of all the people on the farm, he ranked near the top of my least favorite list.

Surprised, I stammered, "Hi, Larry, can I speak to Sandy for just a minute?"

Without hesitating, he said, "No," and shut the door.

I stood there in the dark hallway for a few seconds, trying to comprehend what had just happened before walking back to my room.

Angry and embarrassed, I entered our dismal apartment with my Declaration of Independence in my hand, wrinkled and unread. I had been defeated again without so much as raising my voice in protest. In the corner of the room, beside the bed, I spotted the H&R 12 gauge shotgun that I had used down south on squirrels and rabbits. The long black barrel and smooth wooden stock glistened with oil in the dim light. It was only a single shot, but one shot was all I needed. I was going to put an end to all of my misery. Things were never going to change. I'd be better off dead. Then it hit me — *Hell, I'm not going to kill myself, I'm going to kill Boryslaw! He's the one that's causing me all the problems!*

I started working out the scenario in my mind. I would barge into the meeting, blast that jerk and head for the mountains. I would live on deer and fish and sleep in a lean-to.

Yeah, right! Fortunately for me, and certainly for Larry, whatever common sense I possessed took over. The thought, however pleasant at the time, was foolish at best; well, actually, it was outright wicked. I was a little surprised to see the depths that I had sunk to. I'd only been back a week, and already, I was despondent. I decided that I was

Chapter Ten

going to have to deal with my situation the best I could until such time as things either got better or we left there as a family.

Winter dragged on with each day a clone of the day before. It was a struggle to keep the camp going. We were always behind in firewood, and several times a week, all the men and boys had to go to the creek for water. It seemed that something was always broken down: either a chainsaw or the tractor or the sawmill. Of course, that meant that one or more fellows had to stop and try to fix the problem, which left fewer people for the other projects.

Twice each week, church meetings were held downstairs in the tabernacle. On those nights, I would haul a five-gallon bucket of hot water from the tabernacle stove up to the room, so we could all take a bath. The girls were small enough to sit in the washtub, but Jan and I had to settle for sponge baths.

From our apartment window, we could see the bright glow of gas lanterns and the beams of flashlights as people made their way down the slippery boardwalks to the tabernacle. I could hear the door open down below and people walking on the bare wooden floor.

After getting dressed and dumping the washtub, I reluctantly shuffled downstairs to join the crowd. Someone would pick up a guitar and start strumming. Barbara Boryslaw would grab the tambourine, and the meeting would start. We would all stand up, and for the better part of 45 minutes or so, the praise service would carry on. Hands were raised, and the volume intensified. There was singing and shouting and praying in tongues; there were tambourines and guitars and an accordion, and Lord knows what all else. We sure made a slug of noise though. For those Pentecostal types, it was probably kind of like visiting the carnival, but for me, it just wasn't much fun. I always felt out of place during the worship service.

Wilderness Blues

I imagine that for those folks blessed with musical ability, singing was a joy. Some people weren't so bountifully blessed, but they still liked to sing and that's okay, too. Then there were the guys like me. Not only did I not have a good voice, but I was also shy to boot. To make matters worse, I was expected to participate in the praise service. Sitting out the worship service wasn't an option, though I often dragged my feet before entering the tabernacle and frequently found excuses to get up and leave partway through. Frankly, though I hate to admit it, I was embarrassed by all the hoopla. I'm not very outwardly expressive, so I felt exceedingly uncomfortable during the praise services.

After the singing was finished, the preaching would start. It wasn't organized like a normal church where the pastor would get up and preach from a sermon he had written. Heck, no! There were six elders at the time I believe, and any one of those six might feel like they had the word of the Lord that night, so they all sat up front near the podium. There was usually a little shuffling in their seats and whispered conversation amongst themselves to see who was going to speak first. Finally, one of them would stand up to speak, and we'd all settle in for what was usually a long night. They usually didn't have anything written down, so I guess they had no way of knowing when they were finished. It wasn't uncommon for one of the elders to speak for an hour or more before they returned to their seat. Then there was usually a few minutes of uncomfortable silence while we all waited to see if the meeting was over and we could go home or if we had to sit through another sermon. I don't doubt that more than a few prayers were sent heavenward in hopes that the meeting would end. I know I sent my share. More often than not, another elder would get up because they wanted to "build on" what the last one said. At times, there was an almost audible groan from the congregation as two, three or even four elders felt like they had the word of

Chapter Ten

the Lord.

As the evening wore on, the light from the gas lanterns hanging from the beams overhead would start to fade. It seemed to me like a sign that it was time to finish up and leave, but there was always some civic-minded soul that would jump up and start pumping them till the room was as bright as the noonday sun.

Most meetings lasted from two and a half to three hours. It was really hard to take as an adult, so I know it was torturous for the kids. Without fail, as the night wore on and the kids got cranky and tired, there were always a few who would start crying. Lord knows there was many a meeting where I felt like crying myself.

Unfortunately for the little people, there was an unreasonable expectation that they should be able to endure those marathon events with the same patience as an adult. To this day, I'm not sure why it happened, but the normal thing to do if your child acted up in the meeting was to march them out to the front porch and give them a few whacks. Perhaps this was to teach them some discipline, or maybe the parent of the offending youngster was embarrassed because they might appear less spiritual if they couldn't control their kids. I don't know. I found out later that it wasn't just on our farm that this happened; it was throughout the Move – some directive from the father ministry or Sam Fife or someone. Not much incentive for kids to go to church when they grew up.

The most interesting event in many meetings was watching Gretchen Howard reach casually into the box of kitchen matches by her side, light one and wave it vigorously overhead, leaving the smoke of the spent match hanging effortlessly in the air like some blue-white specter. For reasons beyond me, she always seemed to sit behind Seth, the accordion player, who didn't seem to have any problem whatsoever with passing gas in public. It's not like we had assigned

Wilderness Blues

seats, she could have sat elsewhere, but she never changed her position. Maybe she felt like she was going the extra mile in fulfilling the death to self message, I don't know. I kind of wished she'd had a cork in her purse.

Eventually, the meeting would come to a close. The last speaker would sit down, and when none of the eldership stood up after a minute or so, somebody would snatch the guitar and we'd all stand up stiffly. There was a good bit of yawning and stretching. Three hours or so on a hard wooden bench left one feeling like a tractor had been plowing furrows in your back, and I felt quite certain that my butt had developed a permanent flat spot.

The praise service would end, and there was a feeling of relief that you could almost grasp in your hand. Parents with small children, fast asleep on their shoulders, talked with each other while they searched for shoes and coats scattered over and under the benches. One by one, lanterns would be taken down from the overhead, leaving the meeting hall dimmer with each passing lamp until the last one was removed, leaving the room in darkness.

Chapter Eleven

February brought icy winds that turned noses into faucets and made facial muscles so numb that you had to go inside to warm up before you could speak. I swear there were days when I could even hear the ice form on Game Creek as the bitter cold wind swept up the valley.

On one cold February day, as we were all gathered in the tabernacle for a meal, Barbara Boryslaw stood for an announcement. "Family, we are going to be having our first convention soon, and I think that the father ministry would consider it a treat to be able to dine on some fresh clams. Brother Bob Cramer says that there is an abundance of clams on the beach, and tonight there will be a minus tide, so everyone gather back here at the tabernacle after supper. Wear your rubber boots and warm clothes. Make sure you bring your gas lanterns. Buckets and clam rakes will be on the front porch."

"Hmm, clam digging," I thought. "I've never done it before, but it would be nice to try something different."

The minus tide meant that a lot more of the beach would be exposed than during a regular low tide. It would be a good time to dig clams. The rule of thumb was that clams could be eaten in any of the months that had the letter R in it. That meant any of the winter and early spring months. I guess there was less chance of paralytic shellfish poisoning then, though the experts agree that actually, it can happen at any time of the year. On the flip side, there were several local folks who ate clams whenever they felt like it, so I guess it was a matter of who you wanted to believe.

We met as instructed at the tabernacle porch, and grabbing the tools and buckets, started out into the coal black night, men, women and children walking as a group across the frozen mudflats. Circles of light illuminated the uneven

Wilderness Blues

ground as we clustered around the lanterns, sometimes stumbling in the shadows. Beach asparagus crunched under our feet as we went, the short, thick stems woven into the flats like shag carpet.

After 30 minutes or so, we finally reached our destination. The clam beds, normally covered even during most low tides, were exposed and ripe for the taking. Everywhere I looked, I could see spouts of water like miniature fountains shooting from holes in the sandy mud. Anxious to get started, I snatched a hoe and started digging. Within seconds, I had uncovered a clam — it's hard, smooth shell scraping against the metal of the hoe. I felt like a prospector at a gold mine. Tossing the helpless clam into an empty five-gallon bucket, I got back to work. In no time at all, my bucket was half-full, and I was ready to scoot closer to the water's edge and try a new spot. Though the air was frigid, I was sweating something fierce. I was enjoying myself immensely. It was gratifying to see the fruit of my labors so quickly.

All around me, I could see people bent over freshly dug holes, retrieving the clams that were exposed in the mud. Every so often, they would stand and straighten their backs before grasping their hoes or clam rakes and start to work again. In the harsh glow of the lantern light, I could see their breath as it came in contact with the cold night air; the frosty vapor of dozens of people huffing and puffing as they toiled in the night. We were harvesting the seabed, and it was hard work. We had to move fast. The tide would only retreat for a few hours before it would come rushing back in and reclaim its territory. In our zeal to collect as many clams as we could, we sometimes cracked the shells, exposing the pink flesh underneath.

I heard the sound of an outboard engine and looked up. On the far shore across the bay, a number of gas lanterns were twinkling like stars on the beach. Several boatloads of

Chapter Eleven

Hoonah natives had braved the darkness and cold to harvest clams from their favorite haunts. I envied their courage and determination for venturing out on such a dark night, their only landmarks the mountains silhouetted against the dimly star-lit sky and silently wished them well on their return trip.

The area I was in was starting to resemble the surface of the moon; it was pretty well worked over. After digging several holes with nothing to show for them, I decided to move closer to the water's edge. Taking my lantern from its perch on an overturned bucket, I started towards the rim of the beach. A movement in the eelgrass caught my eye. Maneuvering closer, I stooped down for a closer look. It was a shrimp. Apparently, it was attracted to the light. When I stood to throw it back into the water, I saw them — ten thousand little beady red eyes glaring at me. The bay was filled with shrimp. The sight of them started my heart pounding. Now I just needed to figure out a way to catch the little buggers — not an easy task without a boat or net, but now that I knew they were available, I wouldn't rest until I caught some.

Within an hour of our arrival at the beach, the buckets were full, so we started back towards the camp. The return trip was considerably more difficult. With the exception of perhaps feathers or Styrofoam, five gallons of about anything is pretty heavy. Clams were no exception.

My hands were freezing, and my arms ached. Several times I pitched forward, unable to see the dips in the terrain. The trunk of my body was wet with perspiration, while my face felt like I'd been kissing a glacier. I thought for sure my ears were going to crack and drop off any minute. Every few minutes, I brushed my nose against my jacket to try and stem the flow of my sinuses. By the end of the night, my sleeves looked like a company of slugs had been traversing them. To make matters worse, there was no chance to rest. The tide was coming back in, and it wouldn't be long before

Wilderness Blues

the ground we were traveling on would be covered in water.

We finally reached the road that led to camp. With great relief, I deposited my burden on the ground. I, for one, was ready to start lightening my load about halfway across the flats. But not wanting to be the only man there with a half bucket of clams, I had persevered, though not without complaint.

A tractor and wagon took our hard-won prizes to the tabernacle. We weren't quite done yet though. The clams had to be covered in saltwater overnight with a measure of cornmeal thrown in to try and rid them of any sand inside. I'd never heard of that before, but then again, I'd never been around clams.

The next day, after a good long soak, the clams were opened and cut up to be made ready for fritters. They sounded good and looked good, but much to my dismay, they didn't taste anywhere near as good as they appeared. Though they didn't appeal to me personally, I was very much looking forward to the next set of clam tides. Aside from fishing at the creek, it was the most fun I'd had yet.

Chapter Twelve

A few days after the clam digging expedition, I was with the rest of the camp chopping firewood on the beach. We were having a family project – that's when most of the men, women and children combine all their efforts to accomplish one chore. Today, we chopped and stacked enough wood to last a few days. We were going to have a convention, and while it was going on, only the most pressing needs would be addressed. Everyone was expected to be in the meetings day and night, so preparations were made to minimize the day-to-day chores.

The day before, we had done a camp cleanup – getting rid of trash that had accumulated, putting away tools, raking up wood chips and clutter around the tabernacle, things of that nature. We were going to have company, and like anywhere, you want your place to look nice for the guests. The feeling I got though was more like the atmosphere that prevailed in the Navy when we were told that an admiral was coming to inspect the ship. It was all about appearances. In this case, though, it wasn't an admiral that was coming, it was the father ministry.

That was the name of the apostles or traveling ministry that came once or twice a year for a convention. I'm not sure who told them they were apostles or what set them aside from the rest of the eldership. I believe that a few of them may have had previous experience as ministers or pastors prior to becoming involved in the Move of God. Sam Fife, the head honcho, so to speak, used to own a construction company in Florida, I believe. I guess he was also a Baptist preacher for a while, too. His wife was considered a member of the father ministry as well, though I don't know why, perhaps just by virtue of association with him. Another of the principal characters was a pilot for one of the major

Wilderness Blues

airlines. I don't know what he did to earn a place in the father ministry. Maybe they just needed someone else who could fly a plane — who knows. Unfortunately, I never bothered to question anyone about his or her qualifications, so I still don't know to this day. I can't recall who all was considered father ministry, but there wasn't a whole lot of them, maybe a dozen or so.

The beach was a beehive of activity. Chainsaws roared and spewed out a shower of wood chips and clouds of blue smoke. Men with chopping mauls and axes split the rounds of wood, while the women and children loaded it into a wagon. Steam rose from the backs of a team of horses as they returned from a trip to the woodshed and awaited their next load. There was a sense of excitement in the air that was refreshing, though we were doing the same mundane task as every other day. I had reservations about the convention, but I couldn't keep from enjoying the camaraderie I felt on the beach that day. It was to be short-lived though.

The roar of a small plane interrupted our work as it flew low over the trees behind us, banked and disappeared around the point. While we were still staring off in the direction of the plane, another buzzed the camp, dipping its wings and following the path of the first.

"Must be the ministry," someone said.

This started a flurry of conversations about who might be set into the eldership. Elders were set in or chosen at conventions, and since this was the first convention at this farm, there was some speculation as to who would make it. Being made an elder was kind of like being promoted to manager in a small business. Of course, there was no monetary benefit, but elders pretty much had the say over what happened in the camp, and they were the ones who did the preaching in the meetings. To this day, I don't know what the criterion was that determined who was eldership material and who wasn't. From what I could see, it wasn't an ex-

Chapter Twelve

act science. In several cases, it seemed that those who could benefit the farm financially were set in, though I know that wasn't the only consideration. There were some who were set in over the years who shouldn't have been. There were others who, in my opinion, would have been good elders who weren't set in, but what the heck do I know? One thing was certain, I wasn't enough of a team player to ever even be considered for eldership, which suited me just fine. I didn't have too much respect for many of the elders – in fact, I used to insult John Borelli Jr. when he made me mad by calling him a son of an elder.

By mid-afternoon, the father ministry came slip sliding across the mudflats, many wearing borrowed boots. They looked so out of place with their bulky down jackets and fur-clad hats. Goose down wasn't used very much here in Southeast because of all the rain; when it gets wet, it loses its value as insulation, and few people wore fur hats here because it usually wasn't cold enough. They may have been returning from one or all of the other farms up north. There were a half dozen scattered about in Alaska and Canada, and I'm sure the down coats would be needed there.

As soon as the ministry showed up, the eldership came out to greet them. There were lots of hugs and handshakes and shouts of Brother This and Sister That, but I pretty much felt left out of the loop. The elders escorted the father ministry to their temporary residences and disappeared for the remainder of the day, leaving the rest of us to finish the manual labor. I was feeling a little jealous and angry. Though there was always a certain feeling of separation between the members of the eldership and the rest of the congregation, it became very pronounced when the father ministry arrived. It was as if an air of superiority had descended upon the camp, and they couldn't be bothered with any menial tasks like firewood or water hauling. There seemed to be a class distinction, similar to what exists between officers and

Wilderness Blues

enlisted men in the military, and it left a bitter taste in my mouth.

The only good thing about conventions that comes to mind was that the quality of the food improved somewhat. I don't recall all of the meals we had during those times, though I do remember having peanut butter sandwiches, which seemed heavenly. We also enjoyed a piece of fruit or a cup of yogurt, something we never received at any other time, unless of course you were in town and bought it yourself. While the father ministry was present, we ate pretty well, and I enjoyed it, but I wished they could have experienced life like we knew it. I felt like we were putting on a show, which seemed pretty hypocritical to me.

At every meal there would be a steady stream of people wanting to talk to them about some problem or another. I think in a lot of cases it had to do with some conflict with the eldership that couldn't be resolved. I don't know if anyone ever got any satisfaction after speaking to them.

We usually had a meeting the first evening after the ministry arrived. There was a sense of excitement in the air which I didn't share at all. I rather dreaded the whole mess. I was miserable and didn't care to put on any airs to the contrary. There were a few other people who shared my feelings, but for the most part, we seemed to be in the minority, at least on the surface.

At the start of the meeting, Sam Fife would start strumming a guitar and lead the congregation in some song or another. He would be surrounded by other members of the father ministry and of course the eldership, all of whom gave the appearance of having died and gone to heaven. Brother Sam brought a lot of energy to the meeting and sang with a great deal of zeal. Periodically, he would stop singing in mid-song and start speaking in tongues or launch into something that he felt that God had revealed to him. A good bit of what he said made no sense to me, though other

Chapter Twelve

people seemed to be getting something out of it. There was a lot of head nodding and clapping going on, especially by the more religious crowd. It made me feel all the more isolated.

As a man, Brother Sam wasn't overly impressive to look at. He was a little on the short side with clear blue eyes and gray hair that he combed back, exposing a rather large forehead. He wore long sleeve, white shirts that he unbuttoned, exposing his muscular forearms. It was apparent that in his younger days he had been a working man. His dark trousers had cuffs that fell down over his black dress shoes in a style that dated him. Sam had a sober, no nonsense kind of demeanor and even mentioned once that God had spoken to him about being a crab. I couldn't have agreed more. I have no memory of him smiling or laughing. He didn't appear to be a happy man. In fact, he wasn't charismatic at all that I could see, so it's hard to understand how he could have developed such a following.

On more than one occasion, he said things that rocked my world, though not in a good way. At one convention, he stated, "God doesn't love you." Though I think he was referring to the sinful acts of the flesh man, it was kind of hard to take from someone who supposedly heard from the Almighty. At another convention, he gave a sermon entitled "If They Should Fall Away," referring to people who left the Move. The implication was that if you left, you would be separated from God and, I guess, damned for eternity. It was food for thought, and although I hated being on the farm, I didn't relish the idea of being cast into outer darkness either. It was a go-for-broke mentality that left no room for any other way of thought. I just hoped I got some brownie points with God for being on the farm, even if I wasn't totally committed.

In the Bible, the Book of Genesis states, "Enoch walked with God and was not, for God took him." In other words,

Wilderness Blues

he didn't die. For some reason, Brother Sam had gotten the idea that we weren't going to give up the ghost either. We were going to walk right on into perfection, and we weren't going to die, just like Enoch. Well, that sounded good to me, all except the part about walking into perfection. I would have settled for being a pretty good guy. In any event, some years later, Brother Sam died in a plane crash on his way to visit a wilderness farm in South America. After that, we didn't hear too much more about not dying, at least not that I can remember. However, the perfection message was still being preached. In fact, it seemed to be the primary focus over the years, as I recall. It was especially frustrating for someone like me who knew there was no way that I could ever be perfect, and frankly, didn't want to be.

Over the course of the next three days, we had meetings morning, noon and night. Personally, I could have done with a lot less preaching. My body ached from sitting on those rock-hard benches. It runs in my mind that the ministry had folding chairs to sit on, which irritated me even further. I think if they'd had to sit on those benches, the sermons would have been considerably shorter. To make matters even worse, those who were preaching were encouraged by shouts of "Preach it, Brother!" and "What a word!" While it may sound comical now, at the time, I just wanted to puke. I couldn't understand how so many people could appear to have a good time and I could be so miserable.

The last day of the convention, our visitors were invited to one of the elder's homes to have a halibut dinner, which irked me. I would have loved to have eaten halibut. I didn't so much object to the special meal; it was the sense of separation that I experienced that bothered me. I felt like I did when I was a little kid at the holiday dinner and had to sit at a separate table with the other kids, away from the adults. I didn't feel like it should be that way in a Christian community. I just hoped that the ministry had enough discernment

Chapter Twelve

to see through all the superficial preparations that had been made.

Chapter Thirteen

By mid-March, winter was losing its grip on the land. Warm Chinook winds and ever-longer days joined forces to defeat their perennial foe. Out in the fields, patches of bare, muddy ground were poking through the dirty snow, and buds were starting to show on the thin, red tips of the blueberry bushes that ringed the muskegs. The ice floes that had clogged Game Creek broke up and washed out into the bay, melting rapidly in the saltwater.

I had made it through my first Alaska winter; no small feat in itself, but all the more remarkable having gone through it on an end-time farm. With the promise of spring before me, I allowed myself the possibility that things might get better.

There was talk of building several more cabins to relieve some of the congestion that so many families were experiencing. I had no desire to build a cabin myself. To do so would be an indication that I intended to stay here for a while, something that never even crossed my mind. Even if I had the desire to build a home, I had no money for materials. Lumber wasn't an issue – the forest service permitted each household 10,000 board feet per person per year, enough to make a nice cabin with some left over, especially if you had a large family. It was up to the individual to harvest the wood though, which was no problem on the farm – we had the logging crew for that purpose. The difficulty was that things like nails, tarpaper, roofing, windows and insulation were all expenses that the homebuilder had to provide himself. No problem if you happened to be one of the folks that had sold houses or property before you moved here. However, I was as poor as a church mouse, having spent most of the money we had received from the sale of our car.

It was with great joy then when John Borelli (the elder in

Chapter Thirteen

charge of the transportation for the farm) approached me one day with news of employment. I hadn't spent much time with John; he was often in town taking care of business or picking up the mail, a duty both he and his wife, Linda, took very seriously.

John had been a plumber back in New Jersey before he got involved with the Move. Short and somewhat stocky, he had a classic Mediterranean appearance, with olive-colored skin, dark, curly hair and brown eyes. His upper lip bore a scar that made me think that he had a cleft palette when we first met, but apparently, was just the result of a previous accident.

"Brother Tom," he said softly, "I have something I want to speak to you about."

"Yeah, hi John. Hey, just call me Tom, okay? No brother nothing, all right? I don't like to be called Brother Tom, it makes me uncomfortable."

Listening to people call each other Brother This or Sister That really bothered me – it sounded so religious. Being surrounded by so much spiritual lingo anyway, I felt compelled to discourage people from using any pious adjectives when addressing me. I just wanted to be me, not some holy, righteous, spiritual fellow with a title before his name. I didn't want people to be disappointed when they discovered that I was just a plain old carnal, fleshy guy.

John peered at me for a moment with a quizzical look before he spoke.

"Yes, okay. What I wanted to say to you was that Mike Thompson, who owns the fish house, needs workers for the spring and summer. Would you like to work there?"

I spoke without hesitation. "Heck, yes! Absolutely! When can I start?"

"Well, the position doesn't start until May, but in the meantime, Ivar Issacson needs someone to help him get his boat ready to paint. Are you interested?"

Wilderness Blues

Again, I jumped at the chance to get off the farm and make some money. It was no secret to anyone that I was miserable here, and perhaps they were glad to get rid of me for a while.

John spoke again. "You know, Brother Tom – oh, sorry. You know, if you work in town, half the money you make belongs to the farm. We have expenses at the town house, and we are taking care of your family while you work."

I was unaware of the order regarding the sharing of wages, but it seemed fair enough to me. At that point, had the elders said that it was a 90/10 split, with the farm keeping the lion's share of the money, I still would have agreed, just to get away.

Early the next month, as the weather grew warmer, I caught a ride into town with Tim Brown and Uncle Bill, both of whom had jobs in town at the cold storage. I was officially one of the "working men" – a title bestowed on the lucky few who worked in town for wages. We also happened to have a reputation for not being team players, a distinction that didn't bother me one bit.

Someone introduced me to Ivar Issacson down on the cold storage float. His boat, the *Wyoming*, was docked there. He was a tall, well-built fellow in his early 70s with uncommon strength for a man his age. His red hair was just starting to turn white around the base of his neck and ears, and he had clear blue eyes that could see right through you. Ivar had come to Alaska from Norway when he was a young man and had been around boats and fishing all of his life. He was a no nonsense kind of guy, and I took an immediate liking to him.

"Let me finish this cup of coffee, and I'll show you what I want, Tom," he said in a voice that was surprisingly high. I followed him into the spacious galley and had a seat at the table. I glanced around the room while Ivar sipped his coffee quietly. Across from the table was the oil cook stove,

Chapter Thirteen

and two large coffee pots steamed away on top. Beside it was a small stainless sink. On the counter, a dish strainer sat empty, a testimony to a man who liked to keep things ship-shape. Cupboards lined the walls on either side of the small window above the sink, and several brass hooks held thick, white ceramic cups, the kind you might find in an industrial place like a restaurant or hospital cafeteria. Overhead, dozens of nautical charts lay rolled up ready for use. This was a workingman's boat. No unnecessary clutter, just what you needed to get the job done, no matter what that job entailed. Apparently, paint was considered a nonessential in the galley. Every cupboard and drawer was made of wood, darkened from years of use. If ever a drop of pigment had been applied, it had long since worn off.

"Pilot bread?"

I stopped gawking long enough to look up.

"What's that, Ivar?"

"I said do you want a piece of pilot bread?" he asked, pointing to a rectangular blue box on the table. The box said Sailor Boy. I was to find out later that it was a staple in many Alaskan homes. I'd never tried pilot bread before, and spotting an open jar of jam next to the box, I decided to give it a try.

"Sure, thanks," I said and pulled one out of the package. The crackers were much thicker than saltines and not as crispy. There wasn't a hint of salt on them, and had I not smeared an ample amount of jam on it, it would have been somewhat bland. I failed to see why it appealed to so many folks here.

Finishing up our snack, I followed Ivar out the door to the back deck. It was time to get to work.

"Get on the other side of this hatch cover, and let's set it down on the deck, Tom."

I watched as he easily lifted the heavy wooden lid off its base. Grabbing the other side, I strained to raise it a few

Wilderness Blues

inches while Ivar looked on in amusement.

"What's the matter – don't they feed you out there?" he asked, chuckling.

"Yeah, but not very well," I mumbled. I could feel my face getting flushed, from both the exertion and the embarrassment. Here I was in the prime of life and an old man was outworking me. How unsettling!

I followed Ivar down into the hold to get the tools I'd need to start preparing the boat for painting. For the remainder of the morning, I scraped paint in the sunshine. All in all, it was turning out to be a pretty good day. Spring was on the way, I was off the farm, and soon I'd be making some money.

For the rest of the morning, I didn't see much of Ivar. He stuck his head out the door a couple times to make sure I wasn't gouging the bulkhead with the scraper, and, apparently satisfied, ducked back inside.

Around noon we stopped for lunch, just as his wife came down the dock to meet him. She was a slight native woman with straight black hair and a black patch over one eye. She smiled and peered at me with her one good eye.

"Tom, this is my wife, Norma." Then turning to his wife, he said, "Tom is helping me get the boat ready, honey."

Shaking her hand, I said, "Hi Norma, how ya doing?"

She spoke with a voice like gravel traveling down a metal chute. "And how the hell are you?"

As with her husband, I liked her immediately. I don't know if it was the eye patch, the harsh voice or the genuine nature that she exhibited, but she soon became one of my favorite characters in town. I used to go out of my way to greet her just to hear her reply. It never varied. Spotting her on the street, I would say, "Norma, how are ya, gal?" and it was always, "And how the hell are you, Tom?" Never needing any further conversation, we would both laugh and go

Chapter Thirteen

our separate ways. It was refreshing to talk to normal people — I'd almost forgotten what it was like.

Chapter Fourteen

I'd been working on the *Wyoming* for three or four days, scraping paint on the outside bulkheads and was nearing the end of the day when Ivar poked his head out the doorway.

"Make damn sure you get all the paint chips up off the deck, Tom. If it decides to rain, they'll stick to the deck, and we'll never get them off." Without waiting for a reply, he slipped back inside and joined his wife at the table, an open bottle of whisky perched between them.

Ivar was pretty emphatic when he spoke, so I was going to make damn sure I didn't leave any paint chips on the deck. He kept a vacuum cleaner down in the hold just for that purpose. I swept up all the chips I could and dumped them over the side.

Grabbing an extension cord, I hopped down on the float and searched for a plug in. Following the maze of orange cords to the end of the dock, I found the outlet. Unfortunately, every slot was filled. Looking around, I traced one cord to a boat that was tied up across from the *Wyoming*. I hadn't seen anybody working on board for a few days, so I unplugged it. Not hearing any cursing coming from the boat I had just robbed of power, I figured I was safe. "Sure hope he doesn't have electric bilge pumps," I thought to myself, and climbed back over the bulwarks of the *Wyoming*.

Descending down into the fish hold, I retrieved the vacuum cleaner. Back up in the sunlight, I could see it was ancient. Electrolux was written in silver letters on the side with a lightening bolt slicing through the O. There was a carrying handle on the top, similar to a suitcase, and I was almost embarrassed to be seen using it. Its tubular shape made me think of a torpedo with wheels. At either end there were openings for installing the hose.

Seizing a tattered hose, I shoved it into the nearest ori-

Chapter Fourteen

fice and got to work. I was getting tired and wanted to get some supper. Jan was the housemother this week at the town house, so I was actually looking forward to going there.

I finished up, said goodbye to Ivar and Norma and made my way up to the house. On the front porch, there were three pairs of rubber boots. I expected Uncle Bill and Tim's boots to be there, but whom did this third pair belong to? A closer look revealed the name Holden written in black marker across the top. Buffalo Bob was here!

Bob Holden was one of the few men on the farm that I considered a friend. Down to earth and genuine, he was an affable fellow. Most folks would agree that Bob was a handsome man. He had high cheekbones and a square jaw. A band of snow-white hair ran from the part in back of his hair to the top of his neck, separating his straight brown mane like a line on a highway, the result of some childhood illness. The years he'd spent in the construction business had left him trim and muscular, and I was a little envious of the looks he drew from the single gals.

Whenever we passed each other on the boardwalks, he always smiled and said, "T-Texas Tom." Not wanting to be outdone, I started thinking of nicknames that I could call him. B-Bangor Bob. No, that just didn't have a good ring to it. B-Boston Bob. That wouldn't do either – too wimpy. B-Buffalo Bob. Hmm. Buffalo Bob. That seemed to suit him. It was the kind of name that brought to mind the Western hero type. I liked it. From then on, he was Buffalo Bob to me, or Buffalo or just Buff. I almost never referred to him by any other name, and years later, when I called him Robert, one of my daughters had no idea who I was speaking to. She thought his given name was Buffalo.

Kicking off my boots, I stepped inside. "Hey, Buffalo!" I shouted. "What are you doing here?"

Looking up from the outdated newspaper he was read-

Wilderness Blues

ing, he smiled broadly and said, "Tommy! Tommy Toms! T-Texas Tom! Oh, I don't know. I had some business to tend to. I needed to call my mother and check on her, make sure she's doing okay. Then I saw Mike Thompson at the fish house. He needs a little carpentry work done before the season gets cranked up, so I guess I'll work there for a few days."

"Good!" I said. "Maybe I'll see you down on the dock."

After supper, Tim and Bill went down to the fish house to watch television in the office. Though it was considered a taboo thing to do, I sure wasn't going to say anything. I would have loved to watch a little television myself, if I could have gotten away with it, but Tim kept the door locked. He didn't want anyone from the farm dropping in unexpected. Since Bill worked at the cold storage with him and was of like mind concerning the farm, they developed a friendship. They used the office to grab a smoke and maybe have a cold beer away from prying eyes.

"Hey, Tommy, let's go to the Hoonah Department Store and do a little shopping," Bob said with a grin.

I had no idea that there was a department store in Hoonah. They must stay open late. It was after 6:00 p.m., and the other three stores in town were closed.

"Yeah, okay, Buff, but I don't have any money."

"You don't need money. Just go shop around, take what you want and leave. The Hoonah Department Store is the town dump. People here throw out all kinds of good stuff. This jacket I'm wearing came from there – it's a Pendleton. Someone threw it out just because the zipper was broken, so I washed it and fixed the zipper, and it's as good as new."

I checked out his red and black checked wool jacket. It showed almost no sign of wear and tear. If he hadn't told me otherwise, I would have assumed it was new. Why would anyone throw away a perfectly good jacket just because of the zipper? I was to discover later that many an item found

Chapter Fourteen

its way up to the dump for the most minor of infractions. A broken zipper, a flat tire on a bicycle, a flashlight with dead batteries; it was easier to go buy a new one than to fix what you had. Apparently, the local economy was supplemented by government checks, so it was no big deal to replace whatever was broken. A quick trip to Juneau and you were good to go again.

I said goodbye to Jan and the kids and followed Buffalo out the door to an old blue Ford van parked out front. It had bucket seats with the gearshift on the floor. I liked it because you sat higher than most passenger cars, and for some reason, this gave me an odd feeling of superiority.

After he got seated, Buffalo put on a maroon beret and checked the rearview mirror to see how it looked. "Where the heck did you get that?" I asked, surprised to see him wearing any kind of headwear.

"Oh, I don't know. I think I picked it up down south somewhere – a leftover from my hippie days."

Bob had been a hippie for a number of years before getting involved with the farm, and had traveled to every state in the union except Florida and Hawaii. He had friends everywhere and could travel across the country without having to spend a night in a hotel. His warm smile and pleasant personality made him a welcome guest wherever he went. His rather unorthodox lifestyle had blessed him with an assortment of amusing stories to share as well. He was a modern day bard, and I'm sure that if he had chosen to, he could have made quite a good living going from town to town telling his tales.

We stopped the van at the bottom of the hill and turned left onto Front Street, the main drag in town. At the time, only the locals knew which street was what because there were no street signs. Trailing a cloud of dust behind us, we drove slowly past the unpainted houses on the left hand side of the road. Fires had gutted several places sometime in the

Wilderness Blues

past, and I couldn't understand why they hadn't been razed or rebuilt.

Looking out the passenger window, I could see a dozen or more skiffs scattered along the beach below, tethered to rusty engine blocks or boulders. Quite a few of the locals fished out of these small fiberglass boats, frequently taking them long distances across Icy Straits and beyond – a throwback, I guess, to their ancestors who used to travel far and wide in wooden canoes.

We crept past the Hoonah Liquor Store. It was one of the newer buildings in town, and judging by the line that was forming out front, one of the more popular places to visit. A large, white sign with a capital R planted squarely in the middle shouted from the rooftop, inviting patrons to purchase their cold Ranier Beer here.

Across the street from the liquor store, located in a small triangle of land, was a steel tower, about 20 feet high with a horn on top.

"What's that, Buffalo?"

"Oh, that's the fire siren. Whenever there's a fire in town, someone rings that thing, and the whole town turns out to fight it. About half the time though they can't get the fire truck to start. It's older than the hills. I think the town inherited it from Juneau after they got a new one."

We continued on through downtown Hoonah, past the B.M. Behrends Bank and the old Hoonah Hotel, a ramshackle two-story wooden building with the last remnants of red paint clinging to its vertical siding. The only resident was an old fisherman/shipwright named Charlie Tubbs. He was a bachelor with lots of time on his hands, and if he cornered you somewhere, there was no way to escape him. He had by far the foulest language that I had ever heard. To make matters worse, he always smoked a pipe filled with the most disgusting blend of tobacco imaginable; it smelled like he'd lit a turd in that pipe.

Chapter Fourteen

Traveling on, we cruised past the darkened windows of the See's Greenwald Store and L. Kane's. As we slowly made our way through the town, we passed small groups of young ladies standing along the roadside, and without fail, our approach caused a great deal of excitement as they poked each other and pointed at the van, smiling and waving at Bob. He smiled and waved back, and for all the world, I felt like I was in the lead float of a parade with the grand marshal.

We passed by the Presbyterian Church, its brilliant white painted exterior a stark contrast to most of the rest of the buildings in town. There was a small tower on the roof that housed a large brass bell that was rung vigorously on Sundays and whenever someone died. In the churchyard sat an assortment of old playground equipment, apparently some castoffs from the school. The Presbyterian Church was the only place that I had seen thus far with any semblance of a lawn. Most of the houses were located on small lots. Salmonberry bushes and castoff appliances filled many of the yards, so the churchyard became the playground for lots of the smaller kids.

Next to the church was the ANB Hall, the largest building in town at the time, aside from the school. It was a huge, two-story building built back in the 40s and was used for a number of different purposes — native corporation meetings, memorial services and an annual Christmas Eve celebration. It was large enough to accommodate the entire town. In the years before television came to Hoonah, dances used to be held there, with a live band.

"Did I ever tell you about the time I was in a van like this coming up through Canada?" Buff asked.

"No, I don't think so," I said, scooting around in my seat to face him. I knew I was about to experience a classic tale, and I didn't want to miss any of it.

He chuckled, slapped his knee and started in.

Wilderness Blues

"I was down in Portland, shacked up with this gal. We were in bed watching some nature show about bees. They happened to mention that some people have allergic reactions to bees; you know, swell up and sometimes die if they don't get a shot or something. Well, I had never been stung before, so I didn't think much of it. The next day, I left Portland by myself and was tooling through Canada, in the middle of nowhere, when some bee or wasp or something bounced off the van I was driving, came right into the vent window, landed on my neck and stung me. My God, I didn't know what to do! All I could think about was that darn show I had watched the night before. I didn't know if I should pull over to the side of the road and die or drive like crazy for the nearest town and hope I made it to the hospital."

By the time he had finished, I was laughing so hard my stomach hurt.

We turned left at a fork in the road, and two blocks later, we were at the Hoonah Dump. It seemed a little odd to have the dump located so close to town, but nothing about my Alaskan experience was even remotely close to anything I had encountered before, so why should this be any different?

Climbing out of the car, we began to poke around the piles of burning rubbish that were strewn around. There was an assortment of old household appliances: washers, dryers, television sets with their tubes shot out. Garbage sacks and cardboard fluttered in the breeze, and smoke rose from the trash piles. Flocks of seagulls and ravens scolded us, then scattered as we approached.

"Hey, look at this!" Buffalo called from behind a mound of junk. He held up an old kitchen stool with a small tear in the seat. "I think I'll hang onto this, maybe put a piece of duct tape on it. It will be fine for the men's dorm. We hardly have any chairs to sit on." He brushed off the stool and

Chapter Fourteen

started back for the van.

"I'm telling you, Tommy, you just don't know what treasures you might find here. Once I found a package that had six brand new pairs of underwear in it. I started to pull them out of the pack, and every pair had been crapped in!"

Doubling over with laughter, tears streaming down my face, I finally caught my breath enough to ask, "Well, what did you do with them?"

"Well, hell," he responded, "they were brand new. They were my size, too, but I just couldn't bring myself to take them back with me. I didn't want Sister Vicky thinking I had a bowel problem!"

At the time, the single ladies on the farm were given the task of doing the laundry for the single men.

Still chuckling, I bent down and retrieved a charred wooden mop handle from the mud and began to poke around at the burning piles of rubbish.

"Good grief!" I shouted, shoving an assortment of blackened cans and bottles aside. "I just found the mother lode, Buffalo!" Beneath the smoldering heap of trash, I had unearthed the unmistakable glossy pages of an entire stack of girlie magazines.

Bob glanced over and smiled. "I perceive that you have a spirit of lust, Brother Tom. I shall probably be forced to report this to the eldership so they can cast out that demon!"

While I knew he was joking, I nonetheless felt a sense of guilt for allowing myself to fall prey to my carnal desires. After all, here I was living in a Christian community and I was up poking through the garbage looking at porno magazines. Not much of a testimony. While I was mulling this over, still flipping the pages with the stick in my hand, I heard a faint noise up on the hilltop. Stepping through the bushes with dinner on his mind, a large brown bear walked out. Certain that the wrath of God was about to be visited

Wilderness Blues

upon me for my sinful ways, I took off running, clearing the burning mounds with ease.

"Thunderation, Buffalo!" I shouted, as I slammed the van door shut. "There was a bear up there!" Whether out of a sense of hysteria or relief, I started laughing uncontrollably.

Chuckling, Buffalo started the van. "Let that be a lesson to you, oh man of much lust."

We were almost out of the dump when I spotted a vacuum cleaner identical to the one Ivar had on the boat, only in much better shape. "Stop, Buff!" I shouted. "I want to grab the hose off of that vacuum cleaner for Ivar."

"Shoot, let's take the whole thing. It might still work. They throw out all kinds of good stuff here," he said.

We tossed the vacuum in the back and drove down to the fish house float to try out our find. I plugged it in, and Bob turned it on. The motor roared to life, but there was no suction. I was getting ready to remove the hose and toss the body when he intervened.

"Hold on a second there, Tom, let me try this before you do something rash." He put the hose into the opposite end of the vacuum, turned it on and waited a few seconds. The motor bogged down and then came to life, shooting a grey cloud of dust and paper out into the air. "What'd I tell you, Tommy? Good as new."

"Hey, thanks, Buffalo," I said, as I carefully placed the vacuum on the deck of the *Wyoming*. "Let's go home."

It was my first trip to the dump, but certainly not my last. On one occasion, I found a plaid Woolrich jacket for Jan that looked like new. I also salvaged a recliner someone had tossed. Fortunately, I got to it before it got wet or had a chance to pick up any odor. It had a tear in the vinyl but worked fine otherwise. I put a chair cover on it and used it for many years afterwards.

Chapter Fourteen

For the first five or six years that I lived at Mt. Bether, trips to the dump were pretty commonplace. Some people had no wisdom about what they picked up and would bring all kinds of stuff to the farm that should have stayed where they found it, but others discovered things that were considered treasures. Though I was always a little embarrassed to be seen rummaging around by the locals, it didn't keep me from visiting every few weeks to do a little shopping. You never knew when you might find something valuable that would make you the envy of the camp.

Chapter Fifteen

Within a few weeks of starting, the *Wyoming* was all painted up and looking spiffy. It was done just in time, too. Tim Brown, one of my fellow farm dwellers, had worked into the position of foreman at the cold storage and gave me word one evening that they needed me to help process the fish.

The pay wasn't all that great, but I liked fishing and looking at fish and learning about them, so it was probably a good place for me to be. It had the added bonus of keeping me off the farm, which was worth almost any amount of money at the time.

Tim, like me, found life on the farm less than appealing. Shortly after arriving in Hoonah, he had found work at the cold storage and managed to keep busy all week long, catching a ride out to Mt. Bether on the weekends. Prior to moving to Hoonah, he had been a salesman for a department store chain. His quick wit and endless supply of corny jokes endeared him to Mike Thompson, the owner of the cold storage, and in short order, he was promoted to foreman.

Tim gave me a quick rundown of the cold storage facility. We walked down the long wooden dock, past stacks of pallet boards and piles of heavy cardboard totes — each capable of holding a thousand pounds of fish — sidestepping the spots where rot had penetrated the planks. The smell of fresh salmon filled the air. Sliding open a large plywood door, we looked inside a dark, damp building.

"Here's the glazing room," he said. "This is where we take the frozen fish and prepare them for shipping." He pointed to a stainless trough. "We fill this with cold water and corn syrup and dip the fish into it. It forms a nice glaze and prevents freezer burn. After they come out of the tank, they're put into those cardboard totes and shipped to Bel-

Chapter Fifteen

lingham."

We continued on, past the generator room, where a huge diesel engine was running full throttle, making conversation impossible.

"What do you use that for?" I asked, once we got past all the noise.

"It runs the condensers for the freezers and the ice-making machine," he replied.

"Be careful there," Tim said, pointing to a section of broken plank. "One of the forklifts almost fell through the other day."

Rounding the corner, I could see the tops of two wooden poles protruding above the dock with wires, ropes and springs dangling from the tips. A troller was tied to the pilings beneath the ice chute, a rather primitive contraption designed to deliver ice to boats. The plywood floor and sides of the lower chute were made to slide into the upper chute when not in use. The whole apparatus was suspended from the dock with lines via a series of pulleys and fastened to cleats on the bull rail. Mounted between two pilings that restricted any sideways movement, the chute remained stationary while the fisherman maneuvered his boat, trying to line up his hatch with the slide. This usually took several minutes while the fisherman adjusted his lines, giving slack or tightening until the angle looked right. Then the dock crew had to raise and lower the chute in an attempt to figure out where the ice would land.

Once the boat was lined up with the chute, the fisherman would direct the workers in the icehouse to send down the ice. The men inside would slide open a metal plate in the floor, and the ice would slide down the chute, sometimes with a great deal of speed — it depended on how long it had been since the last delivery and how low the tide was. If the fisherman happened to be the first person in line for ice, an enormous amount could fall in a short period of time, over-

Wilderness Blues

whelming the men on the boat and leaving them cursing and shouting for the flow to be shut off. When that occurred, the workers inside the icehouse scrambled to close the heavy metal hatch with an even heavier metal pry bar, all the while being screamed at by the fishermen down below.

More often than not though, the ice-making machine couldn't keep up with the demand, and the fisherman had to wait while the guys inside the house chopped at the rock hard mountain of ice that formed in the center and then send it down the chute, one lumpy shovelful at a time.

Tim looked over the side and called to the fisherman down below.

"Hi, Henry, how's it going?"

Henry craned his neck skyward and grasped the boom for support.

"Damn it! Why don't you tell Mike to invest in some modern equipment? Every time I come in here, I have to wait for 30 minutes while you guys monkey around with lines trying to get the chute in position. Then when you finally get around to sending me some ice, about half of it is as big as boulders. How am I supposed to ice fish with that? If Mike wasn't such a good friend, I'd ice up over at Excursion Inlet. They've got modern equipment there – good ice, too! Nice and cold, not like this crap you guys try to give me."

When we stepped away from the bull rail, Henry was still ranting.

Turning to me, Tim spoke. "That's old Henry. He's from Norway – came over here back in the 20s, I think. Good fisherman, but he usually has something to complain about, so don't pay too much attention to him."

We ambled across the dock front where another boat was tied beneath the wooden hoist. A rusted wire cable extended from the hoist to the boat below, where two men in rain pants and rubber boots were busy loading king salmon

Chapter Fifteen

into a large metal container on the deck. On the table behind me a dockworker was separating a mound of salmon by size, his rubber gloves and raingear dripping with fish slime and blood. Small piles of bloody ice lay scattered across the tabletop, melting into rivulets and mixing with the slime before dropping slowly to the deck below. Beneath the dock, I could see schools of tomcod swarming around the pilings in a feeding frenzy, sampling each tidbit that slid through the gaps in the planks. I eyed the whole scene with a growing sense of excitement.

I watched as the next load of kings came up, some so large their tails protruded over the edge of the container. What beautiful fish, all shiny and silver and huge. I envisioned myself out on the dock sorting fish – weighing them up while I chatted with the high-liners, those fishermen who excelled at their trade. Maybe they would invite me to join them on a trip to the grounds, perhaps share some of their knowledge with me. Yes, I had a feeling I was really going to enjoy this job.

Boats were lining up, waiting to be unloaded, mostly trollers – the guys that fished with hook and line. King salmon season was open, and the spawners were starting to run over at Homeshore, a stretch of beach on the mainland across Icy Straits. At almost $3.00 a pound, it didn't take long to make wages if the fisherman had any degree of skill. Many of these fish weighed over 25 pounds, and a good fisherman could catch 20 or more a day if it was a good year.

"Well, that's pretty much the whole shooting match," Tim said. "If you've brought your raingear, you can probably start right away. Just go up to the office and have Christy fix you up with the proper paperwork for taxes."

My first job entailed working on the slime line.

Six or eight people lined up on either side of a stainless steel table with sharp knives and brushes. A man with a large knife stood at the end of the table. Reaching down into

Wilderness Blues

an ice-filled steel cart, he removed the salmon, one after another, placed them on the table and skillfully severed their heads, being careful not to cut into the saleable meat. He then slid them down to the slimers, where we attacked the fish with brushes and knives, removing any sea lice that were attached to the scales and trimming any gills or belly lining left by the fisherman. The work was painfully cold. Dressed in raingear, rubber boots and gloves, we had to stand on a concrete floor while washing the fish down in running water. Just weeks before this water was solid ice, now it had warmed up to the point that it could flow out through a hose, but just barely. I'd never been so cold in my life.

Of necessity, the fish had to be chilled. Once out of the fisherman's hold, where they had been kept on ice, the fish were weighed and placed in bins, where they were iced again until they could be processed. After they were headed, brushed, washed and scraped, they were placed on metal trays and put into blast freezers.

Though I was dressed in a full complement of foul-weather gear, the dampness still managed to penetrate into the layers of clothes underneath, so that by the end of the day, I was chilled to the bone and soaking wet. To make matters worse, I had the added bonus of smelling like fish, which, while it didn't bother me, some people took great offense to, as I was to find out several weeks later.

A few days into the job, I was starting to feel like an old hand. There wasn't much to mastering it. The hardest part of the whole process was trying to stay warm. I managed to strike up a conversation with several of the older native ladies that were working on the table with me and found them to be very friendly and helpful. They seemed to find me entertaining and laughed at almost anything I said. Periodically, they would launch into a string of Tlingit words and amidst glances at me would start cackling again, the caretakers of

Chapter Fifteen

some private joke. Perhaps they found it funny that I was working the slime line with them. With the exception of the header at the front of the table, I was the only man. All the other men were running forklifts or glazing fish or hauling the catch off the boats. Months afterwards, I christened myself Tom Humpyguts, after the humpback salmon we were processing, which seemed to endear me to them. Thereafter, we traded Tlingit insults, calling each other Chow-weis or Bughead. Years later, whenever we met at the store or on the street, we affectionately greeted each other with an insult and a laugh.

A few weeks after I had started working the slime line, one of my boots gave up the ghost. For no apparent reason, the sole of the boot parted company with the upper section. It didn't come totally off, just halfway, swinging like a hinge. With every step, the toe scooped up whatever was before me and shoveled it into my sock, like the bucket of an excavator. This was not only unsightly and embarrassing, but uncomfortable as well. Two seconds after entering the fish house, my foot was soaked with ice water and fish slime. Walking the muddy streets back and forth to work required that I stop every few yards to dump the pebbles that had collected inside. Needless to say, my white socks became a challenge that no detergent could conquer. Unfortunately, payday was still a week off, and I couldn't afford to buy a new pair of boots until then.

It just so happened that the great boot misfortune that befell me occurred during the stint that Sister Ethel was housemother. A member of the Thirty-Niners, she was quite pleased that her red hair had resisted the hands of time, unlike her fellow white-haired roommates. On more than one occasion, she let me know that, in her younger years, her nickname had been Ginger, a reference to her curly, copper locks.

In the years before World War II, she had been a wait-

Wilderness Blues

ress at some of the finer hotels in Ohio. In Ethel's time, waitressing was an art. At some point, before moving to the farm, she had acquired some impressive culinary skills. The men working in town were always glad when Sister Ethel was housemother. She liked to cook, she liked to eat, and she enjoyed sharing her expertise with those who sat at her table. The only prerequisite that Ethel had was cleanliness. Without fail, the announcement "Dinner's ready!" was always followed with, "Make sure you wash your hands."

The old saying – cleanliness is next to Godliness – might well have been her motto. No one dared approach the dinner table without first thoroughly scrubbing up. Even as we pulled out our chairs to sit down to dinner, she would ask again, "You washed your hands, didn't you?" Once she was assured of our cleanliness, we were welcomed to be seated.

As luck would have it, the day after my boot rebelled, a squadron of three boats pulled up to the hoist at the fish house. All members of one family, they worked together in the pursuit of black cod, an oily fish favored by the Japanese. At the time, black cod brought a mere 10 cents a pound and was looked on as more or less by catch or scrap fish. Because the price was so low, it took a lot of poundage to make any money, so the boats frequently stayed out for long periods of time to fill their holds, perhaps longer than they should have. These fish naturally produce an uncommon amount of slime, and after a few days in less than ideal conditions, they start to smell.

On this particular day, I was sent to the grading table to help sort the fish that were coming off these boats, a move that I considered a promotion of sorts. Bucket after bucket of black cod was dumped on the table, sliding down in an avalanche of slime that flew everywhere, dripping from my hat and slapping my face. Working furiously before the next bucket arrived, we sorted the fish by size, tossing them into the carts behind us. By day's end, the sleeves of my sweat-

Chapter Fifteen

shirt were soaked to the elbow and drooping limply from my arms, and the smell of ripe black cod had saturated my clothes, a fact that I'd grown oblivious to.

There was no breeze on the dock that day and the gnats, or no-see-ums, swarmed over us, probably attracted by the stench of the fish we were working on. There was no way to combat them; our gloves were dripping with slime. All we could do was shake our heads vigorously and pray for an afternoon wind.

The day ended with all three boats unloaded and re-iced. I glanced around the fish house with a sense of satisfaction. Cart after cart was filled to the brim with codfish and topped with a fresh coating of ice. Several men with hoses and squeegees were giving the concrete floor a final scrub down, shoving the remaining fish scraps through the trap doors while the scavengers below circled like sharks on the prowl.

I hung my rain pants on a hook and started out the door, water squishing from my boot with every step. It was time for supper, and I was hungry. Finding Tim and Uncle Bill at the head of the dock, I fell in behind them as we made our way up the hill to the town house.

"Hoowee, Uncle Tom!" Bill said with a grin. "You smelling pretty ripe there, boy. You better stay downwind of me in case they's any bears around."

Before I could say anything, Tim chimed in. "You know they sell Xtra Toughs down at Hoonah Seafoods, Tom. I think you've gotten all the use you're gonna get out of those boots."

They both started laughing and continued up the hill. Angry at being the butt of their joke, I lagged behind.

"Easy for them to laugh," I thought. "Tim's a foreman, and Bill never gets off the darn forklift. They don't even have to put on rain pants." Life just didn't seem fair.

By the time I got to the front porch, they were both in-

Wilderness Blues

side, sitting at the table. Taking off my boots and socks, I stepped into the living room. Now, whether I was to be pitied or reproached was, I guess, a matter of opinion. One thing was certain, I was a sight to behold. The red flannel shirt that I had donned clean that morning was now plastered to my chest like it had been painted on, the sleeves hanging like damp laundry on a clothesline. My blue baseball cap was streaked with silver-gray trails of dry and drying fish slime, and the foul-smelling goo had even made its way onto my eyebrows and into my hair, where it dangled like ornaments from a holiday tree. Standing barefoot on that cold linoleum floor, one foot was as white as an Easter lily, the other wrinkled and black from heel to toe.

Sister Ethel stood in the kitchen doorway, hands on her hips, mouth agape. She raised an oven-mitted claw and pointed at me.

"Brother Tom," exasperation dripping from her voice, "your clothes are permeating the house. You'll have to get undressed outside before you come in. You can't possibly come into this house like that; we'll all lose our appetite."

From the corner of my eye, I could see my two co-workers trying to keep from snickering.

Frustrated, I shouted, "Well, I can't take my pants off outside, it's light out!"

Stepping back onto the porch, I angrily stripped my shirt and hat off. As I walked towards the bathroom, I heard her comment to the others about my appearance. I wanted to turn around and set the record straight, to let her know how I was the only one that had to work the slime line or grade fish. While those two drank coffee and ran forklifts, I was the one up to my neck in ice water and fish gurrey. I didn't want to come home wet and stinking, but it went with the territory. There were a lot of things I wanted to say, but I didn't. I soaked in the tub and afterwards, ate supper by my-

Chapter Fifteen

self. I could see that it was going to be a long summer after all.

Chapter Sixteen

Spring gave way to summer, bringing warmth and seemingly endless hours of daylight. With each new day, the snow retreated further up the mountains that surrounded the bay, exposing the gray, rocky cliffs and watering the lush, green alpine below. Out in the bay, humpback whales spouted, and men in skiffs trolled back and forth in hopes of catching a salmon. Bald eagles perched in the tall spruce trees that grew close to the beach, scanning the water for any sign of a hurt or careless fish swimming too close to the surface.

Work at the fish house had taken on an almost monotonous tone. Many of the jobs were repetitious and mindless. The hours were long and the labor exhausting and cold, but I was in no rush to have it wind down. As the summer progressed, I found myself looking fearfully into the future.

The fishing season would end soon and so would the money, but that wasn't the worst of it. When my job finished here, I'd have to move back out to the farm; just the thought of it made my stomach knot up. I'd saved up a little cash from my half of the pay, but it wasn't enough to buy a car and leave. Even if it was, Jan was convinced that we had to stay. The constant stream of gloom and doom prophecy from the pulpit was enough to make anyone think twice about leaving. I tried not to ponder what the future held because the present was miserable enough.

Sometime during the summer, Tim had purchased a boat so he could come and go as he needed to. Usually, every Saturday night after work, Bill and I would catch a ride out with him.

Without fail, the three of us would bring boxes of goodies home to share with our families. The quality of the food on the farm had improved only marginally in the year that I had been there. Fortunately, there weren't any more meals

Chapter Sixteen

of brown bear, but depending on who was cooking there was always room for surprises, usually of the unpleasant kind. One person made up some creamed nettles (wild green plants covered in tiny needles that sting and burn long after you've touched them) and served them like gravy over mashed potatoes. Another person got the bright idea of mixing a case of eggs with salmon roe and scrambling it all together. He felt like we needed the extra protein. The chicken/fish egg dish was quite the challenge to cook – the salmon roe burst after a few seconds in the skillet – and it was an even greater challenge to eat. Most of the camp was upset over having a whole case of eggs ruined. We seldom had eggs, and everyone had been looking forward to a treat.

There were lots of stews and soups, and you could count on eating canned fish three or four times a week. The farm spent very little money on food. Flour, salt and 50-pound bags of whole grain cereal pretty much made up the bulk of the grocery budget. All the rest of the food we ate came from whatever we shot, caught or raised in the fields, so there wasn't much variety to be had. It was kind of like having leftovers every day. This led to some speculation on the part of the men working in town. If the money we gave wasn't spent on food, what was it being spent on?

As we approached the tabernacle on our way in from town, I saw Karenna Rawlins, a young teenage girl, passing by on the boardwalk. Mildly retarded, she craved attention from the men of the farm, and would always smile and wave as we came nearer, calling us each by name. Turning to Uncle Bill, I asked, "Have you ever noticed that every time we come in from town, Karenna is walking by on the boardwalk just as we arrive?"

Bill took off his baseball cap and ran his fingers through his dark, wavy hair before he answered. "Yes, sir, Uncle Tom, I surely did notice. Hell, I don't know what the answer is. It's a mystery to me ...a mystery to me sure enough.

Wilderness Blues

Maybe she got ESP or something, but you're sure right; don't seem to matter what time we get off work, she seems to be coming around the corner of that tabernacle at the same time that we coming across the flats."

I found out several years later that she used to walk around the tabernacle about the time that we were due to come home. She would keep circling until we showed up and she got a chance to greet all of us.

My arrival at the farm was always met with squeals of pleasure from my daughters, followed by the inevitable, "What did you bring, Daddy?" I wasn't sure what kind of reception I'd receive if I came home empty-handed.

Within minutes of coming home, I would hear footsteps in the hallway approaching our room. I didn't need to wait for the knock before shouting out, "Come on in, Dick."

Dick Cameron lived in the men's dorm. It was located in the tabernacle, just down the hallway and across from us. It was where all the single men were assigned to live. Their windows faced the mudflats, so they had a bird's eye view of all the foot traffic to or from town. There was no sneaking in with a box of groceries.

Dick was a big man, roughly 6'4" and maybe 200 pounds. He probably should have weighed more, but the farm diet wasn't conducive to gaining weight. He had only one reason to visit – he was hungry. Stooping, he entered the doorway and got right down to business.

"Hi, Tom, I see you just came in from town. Did you uh, did you bring anything to eat?" he asked unashamedly. Of course, he already knew the answer before he asked.

"Yeah, hi, Dick," I said. "Come on in. I've got some baloney and cheese and some Wonder bread – how about a sandwich?" I didn't offer him any of my Pepsi, but I didn't drink any in front of him, either. I only had a few, and they were for my family and me. I didn't mind sharing, but some things were off limits.

Chapter Sixteen

He sat on the bed and talked a little bit while Jan made him a sandwich. His bulk filled the already cramped room, making movement even more difficult. I was starting to feel crowded in my own home.

Dick and I had very little in common. I believe he had been a history teacher before getting involved with the Move. He was plenty smart enough, and if I had been inclined to discuss the Civil War or the Emancipation Proclamation or some such thing, we might have become good friends. As it was, our greatest common bond was that we were both hungry.

"Do you want mustard on that?" Jan asked.

"Yes, thank you," he replied, and then turned to face me.

"So," he asked, "have you heard how the Red Sox are doing?"

He was quite the sports fan and would regularly grill anyone arriving from town for the latest scores of his favorite teams. For reasons I can't remember, competitive sports were considered taboo on the farm, part of that long list of things that only held an interest for carnal people. Sports, like money and education and most other things people held dear, would pass away. They were temporal, a word that was tossed around quite a bit on the farm.

"No," I said, passing him a sandwich. "I'm not really into sports too much. I never have been, unless it was hunting or fishing."

I wished he'd just eat the darn sandwich and go. He was a nice enough guy, not too religious or anything, but not all that exciting, either. If he had some juicy gossip to share, I might have encouraged him to stay, but as it was, he just wanted to chitchat. I think he probably figured that if he stayed around long enough, we'd give him something else to eat. I know that's the way my mind worked. I had been on the farm long enough to know how hungry people think.

Wilderness Blues

Several minutes passed before he finally got up off my bed. I guess he figured the well had run dry. Straightening his jacket, he started towards the door.

"Thank you for the snack," he said. "I guess I better keep making my rounds."

He was referring to the other houses he would visit that night in hopes of filling his belly. A cup of coffee here, a bowl of popcorn there, it wasn't much, but it all helped. That was one thing about the farm. We all knew what it was like to be hungry, and if we had food in our homes, we'd share with those less fortunate, at least most of the time.

One of the single fellows told me about taking a trip to town. "Naturally, I loaded up on as much junk food as I could eat," he said. "I also brought a candy bar home for a snack later. That night, I got the munchies, so I lay awake in my bunk until I was sure all the other fellows in the dorm were asleep. I pulled the sleeping bag over my head and started unwrapping the cellophane as quietly as I could. I was just getting ready to bite down when I heard heavy breathing beside my bunk – I guess I wasn't quiet enough. One of my roommates had heard the wrapper. I guess it woke him out of a sound sleep. Naturally, I had to share."

He was right. It was an unspoken law. You never knew when the tables might be turned.

Chapter Seventeen

The weeks of summer marched by quickly. The run of kings that had been prevalent in May and June gave way to the masses of pink and chum salmon that came flooding into the bays and passes of Southeast Alaska. By the Fourth of July, the floats downtown were full of seine boats, waiting for an announcement from the Department of Fish and Game, permitting them to harvest a fraction of the countless numbers of fish migrating through. Tenders, large vessels equipped with vacuum pumps and conveyor belts, anchored in the bay, waiting to transfer the seine boat's catch aboard before hauling it to the canneries. Boxy-looking scows plowed through the waters of Icy Straits, transporting supplies between Hoonah and the cannery at Excursion Inlet.

Port Fredrick was alive with salmon as they leaped and splashed – dozens at a time. The sheer numbers of fish attracted sea lions and seals, eager to feast on the easy pickings. Seagulls flocked overhead, screeching excitedly and diving on the scraps of any salmon that met its fate. The predators themselves became prey, as small schools of killer whales cruised into the bay, searching for a meal. Any sea lion unfortunate enough to be caught out in the open would never again threaten a fish.

By mid-August, many of the salmon that were previously airborne in the bay were now gathered at the entrances of the creeks awaiting their chance to spawn. The brilliant silver scales that they sported in the ocean became mottled shades of green, white and purple as they entered the freshwater and started to decompose.

In Game Creek, Cutthroat and Dolly Varden trout gathered in pools, waiting for the salmon to deposit their eggs where they could dash in for a quick meal and retreat to the shallows.

Wilderness Blues

Thousands of salmon had already laid or fertilized eggs and were swept downstream where they congregated in shallow pools or along the stream banks. The stench of rotting flesh could be detected long before it became visible and was a dinner bell to a variety of animals and birds. Minks, bears and the occasional marten made daily trips to the creeks to gorge on the spawning fish. Hundreds of seagulls congregated at the mouth of the creek, squabbling with each other, pecking and screaming as if there wasn't enough food to go around. In reality, some were so bloated they had trouble flying. In the trees overhead, bald eagles looked down on the scene below and casually glided to the ground, scattering the gulls and taking their pick of the dead and dying fish.

August gave way to September, and the last of the major salmon runs was peaking. Silver, or Coho salmon, the bread and butter of the troll fleet, were now coming into the cold storage in astonishing numbers. Boats that had iced up only days before were returning with hundreds of fish in their holds, their bright silver bodies layered in ice-like bricks in a wall.

Many of the seine boats that had been tied to the city floats departed for their Southern homeports. Nets and power skiffs were stored and crewmembers were paid their wages, for some the only real income they would see until next year. The local fleet, freshly painted and proud in the spring, now looked tired and disheveled, like men returning from combat. The clean, sharp lines that every vessel displayed at the beginning of the year had given way to scars and rust that stained the planks and ran down the top houses. The season, though short, was intense, testing the resolve of both the men and their boats.

By mid-month, the cottonwood trees on Graveyard Island were displaying their fall colors and relinquished their leaves in a shower of gold to each autumn gust. The days had gotten notably shorter and the rain more steady and

Chapter Seventeen

colder. I didn't need a calendar to know that fall had arrived. Glancing across Icy Straits to the mountains that dotted the mainland, I could see that the first snows had fallen – termination dust they called it.

One by one, the trollers that had been supplying the cold storage departed. Many had followed the fish since spring and were now on their way back home before the fierce seasonal storms forced them to layover in Hoonah for the winter.

With few fish to process and the end of the season looming, I felt like Job when he said, "That which I feared has come upon me." Though I had stayed around long enough to help with the end of the year preparations and milked it to the very last part, my job in town ended and with it my excuse for being there. With a knot in my gut, I caught a ride out to Game Creek. Winter would be upon us soon, and the very thought of having to ride out another one at the farm gave me the willies.

Chapter Eighteen

For the next month, I reluctantly adapted to farm life again. Not much had changed. There were a lot of building projects going on as the number of people arriving at the farm continued to increase. More people meant more buildings, which meant more firewood was needed to heat the buildings. Entire crews were assigned to work on firewood in an attempt to keep up.

Of course, there was also a greater need for food. The fields had all been harvested; they would remain barren until next year, so we turned to the woods. The mountains up and down the bay were heavily forested with old growth spruce and hemlock, which provided ideal habitat for Sitka Blacktail deer. Though smaller than Whitetails, they were abundant, and the meat was tasty.

There were a number of men from the Ware, Massachusetts, group who had some experience hunting deer.

Several times a week, three or four of the fellows would file out to the point and take a boat across the bay to go hunting. I watched them struggle across the mudflats, rifles slung across their shoulders. In the evenings, they would return, sometimes with several deer, sometimes not, but they always had stories to tell about the hunt. Frankly, I was a little jealous of them. I envied their skill as hunters, but even more, I wished I were a part of their clique. Some years later, I did join with the men in the hunting parties, though without much success at first. I had never hunted deer before and didn't have the experience to draw on that some of the other men had. There were many days I returned with the rest of the hunters, cold, wet and exhausted and without the satisfaction of accomplishment. We were always greeted at the tabernacle by a group of curious boys, those considered too young to be an asset on the hunt. This was the part

Chapter Eighteen

of the hunt I always hated.

"Hi, Brother Norm!" they would shout. "Did you shoot any deer?"

"Yup, I've got two nice bucks in the boat," he'd reply with a smile.

"Brother Bob, did you get anything?" they'd ask, crowding around the hunters and waiting impatiently for the answer.

"Yes, I shot a good-sized doe and missed another one," he'd say.

"What about you, Brother Tom – did you shoot any deer this time?"

"No, not this time," I'd say quietly.

"What did you say, Brother Tom? Did you shoot any?"

"NO! No luck and no deer." I wished they would just go away.

With the account fresh in their minds, they would run through the camp giving a report about the hunting party to whoever would listen. I could hear their squeaky little voices off in the distance as they shouted excitedly.

"Brother Norm and Brother Bob both shot deer, but Brother Tom didn't shoot anything."

Like I mentioned before, there were no secrets at the farm. If you passed gas at 2:00 a.m. down by the pole barn, it would be public knowledge the next day.

We usually left the deer in a skiff until they could be brought in across the flats on the high tide. Then they were hauled up to a shed near the tabernacle, hung up and skinned. After hanging for a few days, the deer were butchered. This usually happened in the tabernacle kitchen, after supper. The deer were brought in whole and laid on a large, flat wooden counter. Blacktails aren't all that big, so usually it only took one man per deer to pack them in. Occasionally, during really cold spells, the deer would freeze solid which made them easy to pack in but hard to cut up.

Wilderness Blues

To relieve the monotony one evening, I went down to watch the butchering crew. I'd never done anything like it before, but it didn't seem too hard. Separate the two hindquarters where the ball and socket meet, lop off the front quarters close to the rib cage, cut out the tenderloins inside the belly cavity and make two cuts on either side of the backbone for the back strap – nothing to it. Soon, I'd donned an apron, grabbed a sharp knife and was shoulder to shoulder with the other butchers. It was a skill that I put to use years later after we left the farm.

Alaska has a liberal deer-hunting season, stretching from August to December, with a bag limit at the time of four deer per licensed resident hunter. I'm not sure how many deer we took that year, but it seemed to be substantial. Even so, there never seemed to be any meat on the table. The farm had swollen to over 120 souls, so the meat didn't go very far.

It was early November when John Borelli approached me with another offer of work. It seemed that there was an opening at Hoonah Seafoods for someone with retail experience – would I be interested? He didn't need to ask twice. I wasn't looking forward to being away from Jan and the girls again, but I wasn't sure I could make it through another winter on the farm, either.

With mixed feelings, I packed my clothes and caught the next boat to town.

Chapter Nineteen

I spoke to the manager of Hoonah Seafoods, a Mexican fellow named Jess, and was hired on the spot. People with retail experience were rare in Hoonah, so I had no problem getting the job.

I wasn't sure how well I would be received. Not only was I white, but I was one of those "Farmers" as well. Fortunately, I had gotten to know several of the native ladies while working on the slime line at the cold storage, so I was able to strike up a conversation with them when they came in shopping. Once the ice was broken, it didn't take long before I was on a first name basis with most of the town. In a village of only about 800 people, it's not all that hard. Eventually, I became accepted by most of the locals and developed some long-term friendships with many of them.

As I became more familiar with the townsfolk, I noticed that almost no one shopped for more than a couple days worth of groceries. Certain people I saw in the store every day – sometimes three or four times. I came to realize that the grocery store was a kind of meeting place, like a coffee shop.

Winter progressed, bringing with it a steady string of storms. Cold fronts passed through and dumped inches or feet of snow, only to be replaced days later with rain – bone-chilling, wind-driven, icy-cold rain, in such amounts that days of snow could be eradicated almost overnight.

Out in the bay, angry whitecaps hurled themselves at the beach, pounding on the rocks with a thunderous noise. Travel back and forth to the farm was restricted, and there were more than a few Sundays that I had to stay in town because of weather.

After a couple of times of being unable to get back to

Wilderness Blues

see Jan and the kids, I decided I needed to get a boat. I didn't want to have to count on anyone for transportation when spring came. Having my own boat would allow me to set my own schedule. It gave me a certain amount of freedom that I longed for. Also, I had been talking to some of the local skiff fishermen. There were salmon to be caught in the bay, and for a small investment in gear and licenses, I could be a commercial fisherman. I'd never really given it much thought before, but the idea that people would pay me to catch fish sounded appealing.

Hoonah Seafoods did business with a number of boat distributors in Seattle, and after looking at several designs and prices, I placed an order. I opted for a Hi-Laker, a lightweight fiberglass boat with high lap-strake sides and a windshield. It was 14 feet long and light enough to make the trip to the farm in 20 minutes, if the weather was good. I bolted a 15-horse Evinrude outboard on the back, powerful enough to make the boat plane over the water, but small enough to slow down to trolling speed without stalling.

Throughout the winter, I spoke about salmon fishing to anyone who would listen. Some fishermen guarded their secrets as if it were a matter of national security. However, most of the local anglers seemed willing to impart their wisdom to me. The problem was that I frequently got conflicting information. One fellow would swear that he was catching big kings on chartreuse Pink Lady divers with a whole herring at three fathoms; however, when I mentioned this to another fisherman, he would adamantly insist that the fish he was catching hit strip baits trolled behind a flasher at two fathoms. It was all quite confusing. The end result was that I bought massive amounts of gear in order to be prepared for whatever the fish wanted.

By March, the winter was starting to loosen its grip. I was anxious to try out my new boat and fishing gear and went out after work every evening when conditions permit-

Chapter Nineteen

ted. It wasn't until April though that I caught my first king salmon. Well, I didn't really catch it, but I did have one on the line.

The day was bright and sunny, and the water was like a mirror. Not a ripple disturbed the surface. For reasons unknown, I was alone out in the bay; there wasn't another boat in sight. The skiff slipped effortlessly through the water, leaving a thin trail of blue smoke swirling in its wake. The day was so nice I decided to venture beyond the cannery, to Point Sophia. Though it was only a mile or so further, I was nonetheless intimidated by the very thought of motoring too far from town, in case the weather got foul.

Spring was in the air, and nature was responding. Ravens exploded from the spruce and hemlocks that lined the shores, squawking and squabbling as they chased each other through the branches in their mating rituals. Overhead, groups of bald eagles caught updrafts as they circled higher and higher like great winged kites, until they were just little specks, barely visible against the white clouds.

Out in the bay, massive schools of herring, hundreds of thousands strong, were moving into their spawning grounds. Flocks of black fish ducks dove on the herring, driving them to the surface where gulls swept down, screeching, and scooped them up in a single swallow.

It was a perfect day for fishing, and I was feeling content as I soaked up the rare sunshine. I sat in the back, steering the boat and smoking a cigarette. I'd started smoking again, whole-heartedly. I had never wanted to quit in the first place and had only done so because it was taboo on the farm. Now that I spent most of my time away from there, it was easy to fall back into old habits.

The boat was hugging the shoreline as I made my way closer to Outer Point. The beach there dropped off rapidly, and the water was several fathoms deep close in to the shore. I was approaching a small reef when I saw a V form

Wilderness Blues

on the surface of the water ahead of me. Seconds later, a school of herring shot out of the water, desperately trying to escape from the large king salmon that followed. When he surfaced, his purple back and silver sides glinted in the sunshine.

I turned the boat and started praying. I wanted to catch that fish so bad, I could taste it. In less than a minute, my prayers were answered. The seven-foot rod that had been hanging straight over the side of the boat developed a severe bow, and the reel started screaming in protest. Putting the engine in neutral, I jumped up and grabbed the rod. My heart was pounding so hard that I could hear it. As I stood there grasping the bucking rod, I noticed my knees were knocking together. I had never caught a fish like this before. The only thing greater than the excitement I felt was the fear of losing this magnificent salmon, so I started praying. Like thousands of people before and since, I made a pledge, sure that the sacrifice I was willing to make would guarantee the desired outcome.

"Oh, God," I said out loud, through a mouth as dry as dust. "Lord, if you'll just let me catch this fish, I promise I'll quit smoking."

It seemed like a reasonable prayer at the time, sincere and down to earth. I wasn't asking for anything earth shattering, I just wanted to catch this fish; however, it wasn't to be. Now, I don't fault God for not answering me as I wanted. I have to admit that I was a novice when it came to salmon fishing and not all that knowledgeable about the equipment that I was using. Throw in the fact that I was in a state of excitement that bordered on panic and it was no surprise that I lost the fish. In fact, it would probably have taken a miracle from above to land it.

The king was large and powerful and was taking out line at a startling rate. In my flustered state, I was sure it would empty the spool if I couldn't get it turned. Unfamiliar with

Chapter Nineteen

the star drag on the reel, I turned it the wrong way, making it even looser. Not sure what to do next, I flipped up a lever allowing the reel to freewheel and let out line faster than before. Alarmed at the rate that I was losing line and unable to control it, I slammed my thumb down on the rapidly spinning spool. That was a mistake. The top layer of skin was peeled off before I knew what was happening. Alternately cursing and praying, I dropped the rod to the deck of the boat and started pulling the monofilament in hand over hand, in a desperate attempt to retrieve some of the line. The fish surfaced once, as if to say, "Here's what you won't be showing off." Then the line went slack. I pulled it as fast and hard as I could, hoping that the mighty king was just making a run to the boat, but as the line coiled and curled in a tangled mess in the bottom of the skiff, I realized he was gone.

My first king salmon had escaped. As the reality sank in, a knot began to grow in the pit of my stomach. In a few short moments, I had been transported from the pinnacle of success to the abyss of failure. The disappointment was palpable. I slunk down to the seat and looked out over the bay, replaying again and again the sight and feel of that magnificent fish and the colossal blunder that cost me my trophy.

After what seemed like a very long time of feeling sorry for myself, I picked up the rod and began to wind the line onto the reel. "At least I don't have to quit smoking," I thought to myself, remembering my promise to God. Lighting a cigarette, I reached for the pull cord and started the outboard. I was too disappointed to try to fish anymore today. Besides, there was no good reason for me to miss church at the farm; with the weather being so good and all, I couldn't use that as an excuse.

When I returned to work the next day and gave an accounting of my fishing adventure, I was a little surprised by the lack of sympathy that was expressed. What had been a

Wilderness Blues

major traumatic experience for me was no big deal to everyone else.

When I told my sad story to the husband of one of my fellow workers, he just laughed. Several weeks later, when I lost two more kings, he started calling me "No Fish Tom," a title that really grated at my pride. Almost every day for several years, he greeted me by my new nickname. I made a point of letting him know about each and every fish I caught thereafter for quite a long time, but it didn't matter. To him, I was now No Fish Tom and though I wasn't superstitious, there were days when I wondered if he hadn't unknowingly cursed me.

Chapter Twenty

Somehow or other, word got around about the farm. It could have been the airplane crash that Amanda Harrison was involved in. She had been my landlord in Charleston and was at least partly responsible for me coming to Game Creek. She and some ministry from the other farms were involved in a plane crash on one of the islands, near Juneau. Accidents involving airplanes aren't all that uncommon in Alaska. In fact, I survived one myself, but that's another story. Anyway, Amanda and another lady made it out of the burning wreckage and had to climb down a mountain in this remote location, where they were rescued by a fisherman who just happened to be in the area when they climbed out of the brush. Unfortunately, at least one of their companions was killed.

Of course, the newspaper got wind of it, and later, one of the Juneau radio stations did an interview with her on the air. Shortly thereafter, guests started arriving – not many, just a few curious folks who had read the paper or heard the interview on the radio.

One of the earliest visitors was a young couple that passed themselves off as husband and wife and pitched a tent on the muskeg in front of the tabernacle. We found out later that they were only living together, a definite no-no at Mt. Bether. She seemed friendly and stepped right up to the plate, helping the ladies in the kitchen. But as I recall, he never really pulled his weight, and instead, spent his time gathering eagle feathers and making arrows out of cedar. He told some pretty tall tales about paddling a canoe through Canada and living with the natives there. I can't remember all the details of his stories, but what I do recall sounded pretty far-fetched. They left after a month or so. The farm wasn't the kind of place that appealed to panhandlers too

Wilderness Blues

much.

There was another fellow that showed up a few years later, a middle-aged guy who said he had read about the farm in an old magazine article at the library. He claimed his name was Roland Megow, a salesman for a company that made sandwiches for infrared toasters, the precursor to microwaves. Both his name and his occupation seemed somewhat suspect, but I'd developed a fairly skeptical nature by then, so I didn't trust what too many people said. As it was, my suspicions were well founded. A receipt was found in his room for a brace of 9-millimeter pistols made out to a name other than the one he was using. When confronted, he admitted that he wasn't who he claimed to be. The elders asked him to leave. There was some speculation that he was on the run from a gambling debt or some such thing and was hiding out at the farm, but I guess we'll never know for sure. It was a little scary to have these strangers showing up on our doorsteps uninvited, but our lifestyle seemed to attract a certain segment of the population, though I think they were more interested in the pioneer way of life than the religious aspect.

There was one man, a freelance writer, who came out several times during my stay there. He was pretty well smitten with the place. He wrote quite a nice article about the farm, complete with some beautiful pictures that were published in the in-flight magazine for Alaska Airlines. When I got done reading it, I almost didn't recognize the place. It sounded like the kind of place that I might want to live, except that I was living there already. Of course, he didn't spend enough time on the farm to really get to know it or the article would have been much different. Of course, if he had written a less than glowing report, I doubt that he would have been invited back.

Whenever guests showed up for a visit, the eldership took charge of showing them around. None of the guests

Chapter Twenty

were permitted to just wander off by themselves. There was a certain amount of wisdom in that. Some areas were dangerous. Also, the farm was private property, not a tourist attraction; nonetheless, it was hard to get an accurate picture of life on the farm with an elder as a tour guide. Personally, I felt like I should have had a crack at showing them around, to kind of balance out their views, but that never happened.

One of the more intriguing visitors to Mt. Bether was actually a group of three semi-elderly folks, looking for adventure, I guess. Either that or they had escaped from a mental ward somewhere and were searching for a place to hide. There were two men and a woman, all gray-haired and looking somewhat unkempt, like they had just awoke in the backseat of a van. They had just gotten off the ferry and were walking down the main street in Hoonah, carrying an assortment of backpacks and Army surplus duffle bags, when I ran into them. I made the mistake of saying hi.

The woman spoke first. She had a bossy attitude that really turned me off. I took an immediate disliking to her. "Hi," she said. "You got a boat?" Her question caught me off guard, so I hesitated a few seconds before answering.

"Yes," I replied cautiously, "a 14-foot Hi-Laker."

"Well, we want to do a little bit of looking around. The man on the ferry said Flynn Cove was a nice spot for camping. Can you take us there?" She stared at me with steely blue eyes that demanded an answer.

I looked at her two companions. The one looked harmless enough. He was a fairly big fellow with a huge beer belly. His wrinkled short sleeve shirt hung limply on his large frame, exposing a dirty undershirt and a mound of curly, grey chest hairs. He was nervously trying to build a cigarette, his thick fingers fumbling with the paper as tobacco spilled on the ground.

I glanced over at the other man in the trio. He appeared to be the youngest of the three. He sported a goatee on his

Wilderness Blues

large, round face, and his narrow eyes kept darting back and forth as if he were sizing me up. He kept kicking at a little dog that ran around his legs yapping.

"I don't know where Flynn Cove is," I answered truthfully. Then to change the subject, I asked, "What's the dog's name?"

"Booger," the big fellow answered happily. "Yep, that's ol' Booger. Ol' Booger dog. C'mere Booger! C'mere Booger dog!" He had a booming, deep voice that sounded like he needed to clear his throat.

At the sound of his name, the pooch started dancing and yapping louder, jumping high toward the big man's arms. I didn't know whether to laugh or run. What kind of a person names their pet Booger?

The man with the goatee looked annoyed and swore under his breath. The lady didn't look any too happy, either.

"Where can I find a boat to take us to Flynn Cove?" she demanded.

Unwilling to spend more time in their company, I directed them to the city float in hopes that some unsuspecting fisherman might take them to their destination and I'd never see them again.

While at the town house, I mentioned my encounter with the strange group, and we all kind of laughed about the dog's name, but that was the last I thought about them.

After work that evening, Bill, Tim and I were on our way to the farm in our skiffs. Rounding Game Point, I noticed smoke in the woods near where we store the canoe. I pulled up alongside Bill's boat so he and Tim could catch a ride to the beach and retrieve the canoe.

"What's going on with the fire, Bill?" I asked. "Are the kids having some kind of campout or what?"

Bill took his baseball cap off and scratched his dark, curly hair before answering.

"Damned if I know, Uncle Tom. Sandy didn't say any-

Chapter Twenty

thing about the elders letting the kids go out camping by theyselves."

I motored closer to the beach and shut off the engine. As the boat skidded to a halt in the sand, a little brown varmint came scurrying from the woods, barking and hopping around like a windup toy. Before I could even comprehend what was happening, I heard a deep, gravel-like voice holler from the woods.

"Booger! C'mere Booger dog! You get your butt back over here!"

I couldn't believe my ears. Seconds later, a huge form emerged from the woods wearing dirty khaki pants and a grimy undershirt. He was trying unsuccessfully to light a cigarette in the rain. From where I was at, I could see the tobacco showing through the wet paper. Scooping the dog up, he proceeded to the boat to greet us.

Bill and Tim introduced themselves and walked up to the woods to retrieve the canoe.

"Who's that out there?" a female voice demanded from the trees. Again, they introduced themselves. She walked out into the clearing and gave us the eye.

"You the folks that live at the farm around the corner?" she asked.

"Yes," we all replied in unison.

"Well, that nice man, Jerry, said it would probably be okay for us to spend a few days out here camping. He even gave us a ride out here and said if we wanted to, we could come to some of your meetings at your church."

Brother Jerry. I should have known. Of all the people at Game Creek, he was by far the most zealous. For him, farm life was akin to heaven on earth. He was totally committed to the ideals of the Move and regularly conversed with strangers at length, inviting them out for a visit, perhaps in hopes of evangelizing them, though saving the lost wasn't a priority in the Move. At least we knew how our visitors got

Wilderness Blues

here now.

In the weeks that followed, a routine developed. Every morning, as the men who worked in town reached the canoe, the trio would meet us for some small talk. Booger would run around yapping, with the big guy laughing between bouts of coughing. Sometimes he would help pack the canoe down to the water. He at least tried to be helpful. On one occasion, he came in very handy. My boat was high and dry on the mudflats, and I needed to get to work in town. Tim's boat was anchored at the point, so I figured I could get a ride with him. As it was, he'd left a little early and already had his engine running as I approached the point with one of the gals from the farm. The big guy was standing on the beach, watching the boat leave.

"Oh, dear," my companion muttered when we reached him.

The man turned to look at us and bent down to scoop up the dog. "What's wrong?" he asked.

"Well, I have a doctor's appointment, and I need to get to town, and now my ride is leaving without me."

It was true. The boat had reached full throttle and was almost around the corner. Setting the dog back down on the beach, the man cupped his hands and in a voice like a foghorn called, "Tiiiimmm!"

I couldn't believe my eyes. Though the boat had fully accelerated and the motor was howling, it slowed and turned back toward the beach where we were standing. How Tim managed to hear his name called over the roar of the engine I'll never know, but I was certainly grateful.

The lady came to know the names of the men that worked in town, and every evening as we came home, we would hear her call from her tarp in the woods. Uncle Bill seemed to be her favorite as far as I could tell. At least, that's whose name she always called first.

"That you, Bill?" she'd yell.

Chapter Twenty

"No, it's Tom."
"Who?"
"Tom! It's Tom!"
"Well, where's Bill?"
"He'll be here in a minute."
"Okay."

When the next boat showed up, it would be the same thing.

"That you, Bill?"
"No, it's Tim."
"What happened to Bill?"
"He's coming."
"Okay."

And that's the way it went until all the boats were in and all the men accounted for. It was kind of like a mother hen and her chicks, only not so comforting; for the most part though, they were pretty harmless.

Aside from a few gunshots one night to scare off a reported bear, the only other excitement from their camp was when Bob Cramer returned from town one evening.

"That you, Bill?" she called from the trees.
"No, it's Bob."
"Who?"
"Bob. Bob Cramer."
"Bob? Well, hell, if I'd known it was you, Bob, I'd have worn my black panties!"

Though he was laughing when he relayed the conversation, Bob nonetheless seemed a little shaken. The vision of that old gal in her underwear was enough to send chills up and down the spine of any young man.

Eventually, they packed up their tarp and other belongings and caught a ride into town. I'm not sure where they went from there; we never heard from them again. Though it's hard to imagine, it took a few weeks to get used to their absence. I think I actually missed our welcoming committee.

Wilderness Blues

There were others that passed through from time to time, though none as memorable as the trio I just mentioned. Usually, they were hoping to connect with us somehow ...spiritually, I guess. When it comes to matters concerning religion, there was no shortage of opinions or ideas. Most stayed for a day or two and passed on, looking for someone of like mind. Usually, I was glad to see them go; we had enough strange ideas going on without importing more from outside.

Chapter Twenty-One

Sex. Judging by the world's population, I'd say most of us enjoy it to some degree. I read somewhere that the average male has a thought involving sex roughly once every three seconds. That sounds about right. It's kind of an involuntary thing, like blinking your eyes. Depending on the situation, you can dismiss the thought and concentrate on whatever it is that you were doing, or you can entertain it, in which case, it will eventually be acted upon.

In the book of Genesis, God said to Adam and Eve, "Be fruitful and multiply." In other words, do what comes naturally. He wanted people to populate the earth. When it came to that, Jan and I were doing our part willingly.

Of course, there are ways to prevent pregnancy. Lord knows we tried our share, but the bottom line is, we arrived at the farm with two children and left with seven. Our family wasn't the largest, either. There was at least one family that had eight children, and that was just while they were there at Mt. Bether. After they left, I think they were still cranking them out. When it came to sex on the farm, I think it's fair to say there was plenty of it.

It seems so unfair that the desire to procreate starts long before it is acceptable to act on it. In an effort to contain the natural lust that starts to develop at the onset of puberty, young people at Mt. Bether who were members of the opposite sex were not allowed to be together unless there was an adult chaperone. Theoretically, this would eliminate any potential problems. The reality, though, was much different. There was one young couple who were attracted to each other like the two poles of a magnet. Even under the watchful eyes of dozens of adults, they managed to rendezvous at all hours of the day or night, in the barn, out in the woods, even in the outhouses – not the most romantic places to

Wilderness Blues

meet, but desperate times required desperate measures. They were called in to speak to the elders on more than one occasion. Though they weren't the only young couple to dabble with desire, I think they were the only ones that were ever caught. Eventually, they both left. Whether or not they found each other outside of the farm, I don't recall.

Don't get me wrong. The eldership wasn't against love, or even sex for that matter, but premarital sex was definitely not on the to-do list. Couples who were of age and were in love, or at least thought they were, could approach the eldership and, with their approval, could commence in an engagement period. It was called walking out a year, and as the name implies, it lasted a year, at least. It gave the couple an opportunity to get to know each other better, though I don't know how. The only difference that I could see was that they could sit together at meals and during meetings, without turning any heads. They still had to be in the presence of other adults when they were with each other. I guess it worked. There were quite a few people who married while they were on the farm, and to the best of my knowledge, none of them ever got called into the eldership for inappropriate conduct during the engagement period.

Of course, walking out a year and getting married on the farm was no guarantee of everlasting bliss. Of the 11 marriages that took place at Game Creek between 1975 and 1983, I know of three that ended in divorce after they left the farm. Who knows why. Perhaps they were married because they felt like time was running out and didn't want to miss the chance. The fact is there were only so many young, single people on the farm and not much opportunity to get out and mingle with other folks outside of the community.

In the case of Jason Simms, the only black man, there was even less of a chance. To the best of my knowledge, he never expressed an interest in marrying outside of his race, and like most of the folks there, I just assumed he would

Chapter Twenty-One

stay single. For reasons unknown, the Move didn't seem to appeal to many African Americans. As it was though, two sisters from a group in Detroit moved to Game Creek. From the get go, there seemed to be a bit of competition between the two, with Jacob as the prize. In the end, he did marry one of them. Some years after they left the farm, they also got a divorce.

The only reason I'm even writing about this is because of all the misunderstanding about God, love, sex and Christianity, not that I'm an expert about any of the aforementioned. I just know that, like so much else, there were a lot of misconceptions when it came down to the meat and potatoes of love on the farm. In the final analysis, people are going to be people. Living on an end-time farm, with the end of the world looking us in the face, didn't change the natural desire that God put within us. So, young and old, married or not, spiritual act or just plain carnal lust, sex happened. Thank God!

Chapter Twenty-Two

The obvious result of all the lovemaking that was going on was an increase in our population. It seemed like, at any given time, there were at least two or three pregnant ladies wandering around the camp, and usually, several gals that had a child or two under the age of 3. It was a regular baby boom.

To make matters worse, for the first few years that we were there, there was a steady influx of people moving onto the farm. With only limited housing available, things got pretty crowded. This sparked a building boom.

The Browns were one of the first families to have their own home. They and their three young boys had been stuffed like sausages into an 8 x 10 room. As it was, the boys were bedded in a three-tier bunk, one above the other like a triple-decker ice cream cone. Denise and Tim had a small bunk along an outside wall, and a dresser or two filled up the rest of the space. No doubt, they dressed in shifts.

The general feeling on the farm at the time was that if you wanted to build your own cabin, you were expected to foot the bill for all the building materials, with the exception of the lumber, which was cut right there at the mill. Tim was working in town, so he had some money to buy supplies with.

The house he built wasn't all that large or fancy; I think it only measured 24 x 24 feet. There was no running water, electricity or indoor plumbing; I can't even recall seeing any sheetrock on the walls. Nonetheless, there was a stirring of discontent and jealousy after the project was completed. ("Did you see how big that cabin is? Why does one family need so much room?")

It was a rather un-Christian attitude to have, and certainly not one you would expect to find on an end-time

Chapter Twenty-Two

farm. Many folks might even consider such talk petty, and I suppose they would be right. It's surprising to see what is inside of us. There is nothing like a little trial or tribulation to bring out the beast in you.

Perhaps because of the talk around the farm, or maybe just because they were feeling generous to a friend in need, they invited Buffalo Bob and his young son, Levi, (named after the jeans) to live with them. It seemed to appease the "space police" (those concerned with how much space a family needed to live in before they crossed over the line into carnal excess).

As my own family got larger, we moved across the hallway in the tabernacle to the room vacated by the Carsons, who by then had built their own cabin.

The space we moved into occupied two bays, so we now had a room that measured 12 x 30 feet. It was divided into three parts with the center being the living room. We actually had a place to put a small table and a few chairs, so we didn't have to lounge on the bed when we were home. It seemed quite spacious when compared to our previous two dwellings. I even had room to put the recliner that I had salvaged from the town dump.

Five years reluctantly dragged by, and our family had grown to six. I had four daughters, and we now occupied a third bay in the tabernacle. Leaving the farm, while always in the back of my mind, seemed like less and less of a possibility. I didn't see how I could possibly afford to leave with so many little mouths to feed.

Much to my delight, Jan expressed discontent with the farm on occasion, but I didn't believe she was ready to depart; the fear of leaving was too great. The only practical solution was to build my own cabin.

We approached the eldership with our request. As we entered the room where the elders' meeting was being held, I noticed the group seemed to be divided into little cliques.

Wilderness Blues

Those from the south, the Charleston group, sat together and those from Ware, Massachusetts, and Alaska sat in a different area of the room. Sandy, as always, was a gracious host and offered us coffee, while Larry started a conversation with one of the other elders and did his best to pretend we weren't there.

"You precious folks have a seat," Sandy said. Her voice was drenched with Southern charm as she handed us each a steaming cup. "You mentioned you wanted to build a cabin for your delightful little family, Brother Tom?" she continued.

I wish she hadn't called me brother. It actually hurt a little bit. She always called me Uncle Tom whenever we were in a less formal setting, and though it sounded a little goofy, it was a term of endearment. When she was with the rest of the eldership though, she put on her elder persona, which seemed less friendly and Sandy-like.

Jan sat quietly beside me, sipping her coffee while I spoke. I don't like speaking in public, and while I wasn't exactly giving a speech at the United Nations, I was still uncomfortable. Being around a group of elders can be pretty intimidating.

"Yeah," I started nervously. "We'd like to put up a cabin at the end of the property line, in the woods looking out over the fields. My family is getting big, and the tabernacle is getting a little too small for all of us."

There was some polite laughter, and a few heads shook knowingly, as I searched my mind for more excuses that would enhance my case. I didn't want to mention the noise we had to tolerate on a daily basis from the endless traffic down below, or the fact that privacy was almost nonexistent there. Then there was the fact that my kids couldn't be kids in their own home. In the end, not much convincing was needed. Everyone pretty much agreed that if we were going to stay, we needed our own cabin. Then they laid the bomb-

Chapter Twenty-Two

shell on me.

Velma Lawrence did the talking. She was an attractive, middle-aged, petite woman with salt and pepper hair cut short and full lips that couldn't quite hide her front teeth when she closed her mouth. She was by far the most business like in the group, and I respected what she had to say.

"You know, Tom, you'll have to provide any of the building materials needed for the cabin. If you submit a lumber list to the sawmill, they will do their best to provide the necessary wood, but keep in mind, there are other building projects going on, too, so you may have to wait."

"Yeah, I'm aware of that," I replied.

"Also, you and Jan will have to sign a resident's agreement."

"A resident's agreement. What's that?"

"It's a legal document stating that if, for any reason, you should leave the farm, you give up all rights to your home. The cabin becomes the property of Mt. Bether."

It was the first time I'd ever heard anything like this. My guts started churning like they were full of last night's sauerkraut. They had me over a barrel. We needed to find a new place to live, but if I built it, it wouldn't really be mine. The thought of walking away from a home that I had invested time and money in didn't rest well with me, but I didn't feel like I had a whole lot of choice, so I agreed to sign.

Later, Uncle Bill told me that the reason for the legal paperwork was to prevent the farm from being sued. Apparently, a fellow who had been living at the Haines farm became dissatisfied with things or angry at the eldership or some such thing and demanded all of his money back. I guess he had quite a substantial investment in the place, and in order to keep it out of the courts, the farm had to scramble to get him his money. It just about closed down that farm, at least that's what I'd heard.

Now, I don't know who all signed that document; I was

Wilderness Blues

under the impression that it was mandatory for anyone who wanted to build his own place. However, I do know of several disgruntled families who threatened to cut out all the windows or burn down their cabins if they weren't compensated before they left.

To the best of my knowledge, all of the cabins remained intact, so I assume that some money exchanged hands, but I never really heard.

In February of 1981, we started building our own home. My dad, who was a contractor, sent me a book of house plans so I could get some ideas for our cabin. I didn't want to have just some square, ordinary building; my place was going to give people something to talk about. As I searched for a house plan, I ran across one that really caught my eye — it was named, appropriately enough, The Rebel. It had a balcony and greenhouse that cantilevered off the second floor, and it really gave the place a look of class.

I don't remember how long it took to build — maybe six months or so. There was a crew of three or four working on it off and on, depending on what other needs there were on the farm. Due to its location, it was more of a challenge to build than any of the other cabins. There was no road to the lot, so all the materials had to be delivered by horse or tractor to a field out front and packed up a small hill. In one case, we loaded a barge and floated the supplies in on a very high tide. After the water receded and the barge set down on the fields, the real work started. All the particleboard, sheetrock, steel roofing and lumber had to be hauled up to the building site. The roof rafters were the most miserable to pack: 22 feet long and green, they weighed a ton. There was such a demand for lumber that it never had a chance to season.

Grabbing two rafters at a time, with a man on each end, we started hauling them up to the site. The boards were so lengthy that they flexed in the middle and bounced on our

Chapter Twenty-Two

shoulders like a kid on a trampoline. To make matters worse, the ground was muddy and laced with multitudes of tree roots that tripped us up. Slipping and stumbling and jerking along, we fought our way to the top and dropped our loads, looking back at the barge to see how many more trips up that dreadful rise we had to make. Though the hill was relatively small, maybe 20 feet high, by the time we were finished, I felt like a Sherpa on an expedition up Mt. Everest.

By midsummer, the house was completed, and we moved in. It was so nice to have a place of our own and even more pleasant because we were far removed from the other cabins. There was a sense of isolation which I relished. We were surrounded by forest on three sides, so it was quiet and very private.

On more than a few occasions, I stepped out my front door to take a leak. Well, actually, it was a nightly occurrence. There is something liberating about standing on the upstairs porch and letting fly. Not many people have that kind of freedom, though, I would have gladly traded it for a flush toilet.

Yet another benefit of living in the woods was the opportunity to view wildlife. Deer were frequent visitors as was the occasional brown bear. The slough out front was a favorite spot for mallard ducks in the late fall and winter, and once, we had a swan take up temporary residence there, its brilliant white feathers a stark contrast to the dreary brown grasses of the surrounding field.

Otters also took a liking to the pools and spent hours chasing each other with clumsy, slinky-like movements before sliding down the snow and into the water where they were transformed into graceful athletes.

We had been in our new home a few months when I heard a knock on the door one Sunday. It was mid-afternoon, and I wasn't expecting anyone, so I turned the

Wilderness Blues

knob with a bit of apprehension. It was Sister Ethel, the gal who wanted me to disrobe on the front porch so I wouldn't stink up the place with my fish clothes.

"Hi, Brother Tom!" she shouted, smiling from ear to ear. "I thought I'd come visit you, and I hope you don't mind, but I brought a few friends." She gestured behind her.

Opening the door wider, I peeked down the steps. From the bottom of the stairs to as far down the boardwalk as I could see, there were members of the farm. I was flabbergasted! The whole farm showed up to give us a house warming. How we all fit in the upstairs rooms is still a bit of a mystery to me, but we did. We shared coffee and yellow cake and lots of conversation. I don't even recall anyone getting too religious over anything. For me, it was a milestone event. For the first time ever, I felt like I belonged here.

Chapter Twenty-Three

Shortly before our cabin was finished, the farm purchased a generator. We finally had electricity. With surplus wire purchased from the local power company, a couple of the more knowledgeable fellows started stringing lines around the camp – first to the tabernacle and sawmill, then to the various cabins and the barn.

With a generator in place, we were able to set up a pump station down by the creek, so we wouldn't have to pack water anymore. First, though, we had to install water lines, which in itself was a major undertaking. The lines had to be at least a foot underground to keep them from freezing during the winter. This required plunging a chainsaw into the soft ground and moving in the direction that was the shortest distance to the desired building. In a haze of blue smoke and deafening noise, the crew cut a path across the wet muskegs, with water and mud spewing out of the ports of the saw where woodchips usually flew. It was messy work, but everyone agreed it would be worth it.

Progress had its drawbacks, and having a generator, while a tremendous asset, wasn't without its problems. One of the biggest hassles was on church or meeting nights. Many of the women had purchased blow dryers for their hair now that they had electricity. Though it had been explained on a number of occasions that the generator could only handle so many electrical appliances at once, and in particular, those that produced heat, it seemed to fall on deaf ears. Without fail, you would be cutting or sanding a board and the power would shut off in mid-project. Sam, the guy in charge of the generator, would have to stop what he was doing and go fix it. At the next mealtime would be the inevitable announcement.

"Family, as you all know, the power went off again. Like

Wilderness Blues

I said before, if you're going to be using something that draws a lot of electricity, especially blow dryers or curling irons, turn off your lights or check with the building crew to make sure they aren't going to be using any power tools."

Of course, that never changed anything. The same problem happened again and again. There seemed to be a mentality among certain people that they were somehow exempt from the rules, and frankly, there were times when I fell into that category myself. I guess it's just human nature to believe that whatever it is you are doing at the time is just a little more important than someone else's project, whether it's running a power drill or curling your hair.

It runs in my mind that, eventually, at least on meeting nights, that families were assigned definite times when they could use their hair care doo-dads and thus avoid conflict with other power users. It didn't totally eliminate the problem, but it helped.

All things considered, things were getting better on the farm, perhaps in part because of the influx of money that the Alaska permanent fund brought in. Every Alaskan resident was eligible to receive a portion of the profits from the oil wealth, and in the fall of 1982, a check for $1,000 was mailed to every man, woman and child who qualified. This was quite a boost; my own family received checks totaling $7,000. I had never seen so much money at one time in my entire life!

The eldership was quick to point out that even though the money wasn't earned, it was still considered an income, and as such, everyone was required to give half to the farm. I balked at the idea, initially. I had quit working in town so I could build our cabin, so this was the only money I had coming in. However, as I gave it some thought, it seemed like a reasonable thing to do. There were roughly 100 people on the farm at the time, and that would translate into about $50,000 of much-needed revenue. It runs in my mind that

Chapter Twenty-Three

there was a meeting to discuss what the extra money would go to, and if I remember correctly, the eldership was open to suggestions about what needs should be met. It was one of the only times I can recall that we acted like a democracy.

A new tractor was purchased and some chainsaws, and Lord knows what all else. There was even a change of heart concerning the buying of canned goods. Up to that point, almost everything we ate came from the land, with the exception of a few staple items like flour, sugar and grains suitable (more or less) for cereal.

They even let me have a hand in the ordering of the food, which kind of surprised me. I guess they figured that my background in retail could be an asset. Of course, nothing ever went off without a hitch, and such was the case with my placing an order for groceries.

The gal in charge of the kitchen at the time wanted me to order the usual stuff – oatmeal, cornmeal, bulgur wheat and mung beans. We went a few rounds about that.

"Judy," I said, somewhat exasperated, "why the heck do you want to order more mung beans? If you look down in the cellar, you'd probably find a bag or two that have been hidden from the last order you made. No one wants to eat them – except perhaps you."

"They're very nutritious," she replied evenly.

"I don't know how they can be nutritious if you don't eat them," I shot back.

With a bit of color in her cheeks, she responded a little more sharply. "I'm responsible for the meals that are prepared here at the tabernacle, and they need to be healthy."

"Well, I suspect that healthy is a matter of opinion," I responded. "There's no law about food tasting good, is there? Thunderation, this place drives me nuts! Between the rutabagas, the groats and the wheat balls, I'm about to starve to death!"

At the time, there was a bit of a joke going around camp

Wilderness Blues

about the wheat balls we had been eating for breakfast. I can only liken it to chewing rubber cement. They were so pliant that after breakfast your jaws would hurt from all the work required just trying to eat them. If a little peppermint extract had been added, they could have been a substitute for chewing gum. Even my digestive system had a hard time dealing with those balls; most of the time, they just passed through unharmed. In babies and small children, they didn't break down at all. If a small child was fed wheat balls at breakfast, you can be sure that they would exit in the evening looking very much the same as they did in the morning. In fact, it was hard to contain them in a diaper. More than a few times, they fell out and bounded across the floor like a super ball. They were practically recyclable! Lord knows how they affected the elderly gals in the Thirty-Niner's cabin.

"Well," she replied, "if you're dissatisfied with the menu, you'll have to speak to the elders about it."

Needless to say, I wasn't about to do that. I had the order book and the phone number for the wholesale grocer, so I went to town and ordered what I wanted. For the first time in years, I was satisfied with the way things were going, more or less.

Chapter Twenty-Four

Things on the farm were definitely changing. One of the more eccentric fellows started a small store in the back of his cabin. Nothing fancy, just some staples and a few extra things that appealed to the masses. Popcorn was always popular, as was powdered milk and coffee. Being a bit of a health nut, he didn't carry chocolate, but he did sell carob. He also sold these nutritious (or so he said) candy bars made with sesame seeds and honey, Waa Guru Chews. They were encased in cellophane with a picture of some maharishi on the wrapper. I had never seen them before, nor have I since. For all I know, he purchased them at a head shop. They tasted pretty good though – kind of sweet and chewy. They beat the heck out of wheat balls.

The eldership decided that one night a week would be family night when, instead of eating in a group at the tabernacle, families would be given food to cook in their own homes. We weren't given any choice in the menu, usually it was ground meat or eggs and potatoes, but it was a nice change of pace and was universally applauded as a good thing. People with families were encouraged to invite single people to have dinner with them, which helped to establish relationships, something that was sorely lacking on the farm.

Buying the generator had an impact on things other than power tools and hair dryers. The whole self-sufficient, pioneer spirit way of thinking seemed to be altered somewhat. People were freed up from having to manually pack water. Several electric washers were purchased and placed in a laundry house; the ladies weren't forced to scrub their family's clothes on washboards anymore. We were starting to re-enter the 20th Century.

Having electricity meant having more time for recreation, which had been almost nonexistent for the first five

Wilderness Blues

years. Someone bought a used ping-pong table and placed it in the tabernacle. After the supper dishes were all washed and put away, whoever wanted to could play. It gave the young people something to do. The whole thing was a radical change from the earlier years when competitive games were considered taboo. Other forms of entertainment became acceptable, too. Barbara Boryslaw, the fire and brimstone elder (who also wore the hat of school principal), decided to have the high school perform a play from the Book of Judges, one of the books of the Old Testament. It was surprisingly good. Barb was the narrator, reading from a scroll in a loud monotone voice that highlighted her somewhat dry sense of humor. For the first time ever, I looked at her as a normal person, not just as an elder on a spiritual power trip. There was even a talent show. It was amazing to see the amount of ability that had been lying dormant under the ever-present cloak of religious appearance. There were humorous skits, songs, a jump rope demonstration and things that I've long since forgotten about. I just remember that it was fun, a word not normally synonymous with farm life.

Eventually, a family fund was established for those who had no income. A percentage of the money that came into the farm from the men who worked in town was divided equally among the residents in need. It never amounted to much, maybe $20 to $40 a month, but it beat nothing at all. Of course, the small monthly stipend only covered the most basic of needs. Anyone that required medical or dental help still had to get a job and pay for it himself. Nonetheless, change was happening – some good, some not so good.

People were starting to leave the farm now. For the first time since we came, there were more people departing than arriving. There were a variety of reasons. Some folks had realized that this wasn't the place for them shortly after they got here. Most spent a year or more before they finally de-

Chapter Twenty-Four

cided to take the plunge. Almost without fail, they would drop in and see me before they left; I had a reputation of sympathizing with those who were taking their leave. Usually, we badmouthed the elders a little bit and talked about what was wrong with the farm.

There was also another reason people were leaving. There was a rumor going around the camp about this fellow named Fred Vanderhoof. I'd never heard of him before, but those that knew of him said he was a hard-nosed fellow, a kind of enforcer of farm policy who traveled to the different farms and gave people the boot. I found out later that some people blamed him for having their pets put down on a few of the farms up north. I guess he felt that if an animal wasn't working, it wasn't worth having. I don't know how much of what I'd heard was true, but when he did show up, I hated him intensely.

Fred arrived with the father ministry during one of the conventions. Tall and thin, he had a no nonsense demeanor. All he needed was a cigarette and he could have passed for the Marlboro man. I tried not to pay too much attention to him. I was half-afraid he could read minds and would see that he intimidated me.

Before the convention was over, the rumors were flying that several families were asked to leave. I was on pins and needles, waiting to see if we would be next. It was a strange relationship that I had with the farm. Though I despised living there, I was too scared to leave. Aside from the issue of being able to provide for my large family, there was the whole "being out of God's will, going to hell if you leave" problem. Being told to leave the farm was a terrifying thought.

At the time that this Vanderhoof fellow showed up, we had only been in the house for a short time. I figured he'd ask us to leave and then, because we had signed the resident's agreement, we wouldn't get any compensation for the

Wilderness Blues

materials we'd bought. I spent hours fretting over what to do if he asked us to go. I'd pretty much determined that I would torch the place. I sure wasn't going to let the farm have my house if they were going to force me out. As it was though, we weren't asked to leave, at least not then.

With every family that left, my heart ached, not so much because I would miss them – there were some whose departure I rejoiced in – but because I was still there. For those who chose to leave voluntarily, I was envious. They had the courage to go back out into the world and face its many challenges. For those who may have been asked to leave, I was still envious. They were getting off the farm, like it or not.

Chapter Twenty-Five

What is a farm without animals? When we first arrived, there were very few, just a couple of horses, Pete and Joe the oxen, and the two pigs, Adam and Eve. As the years progressed, more animals were acquired. Of course, that meant a barn would be needed to accommodate them. Bob Pinard and his young son, Brent, took on the task of building it almost singlehanded.

With a real barn in place, milk cows were purchased, and it was no longer necessary to buy the powdered stuff for the kids.

In fact, the cows were producing so much milk that the gals in the kitchen started mixing it up with nutmeg and vanilla and serving it hot with toasted bread. For the first time ever, we had coffee breaks and actually had some refreshments to go with them. Surprisingly, there were one or two hard noses that complained about taking time out from the work schedule to have a snack, but no one paid them any attention.

Of course, all those cows didn't milk themselves, so volunteers were sought to do the dirty deed. For several years, I was unwilling to be involved with them. For one thing, they stank, then there was the whole grabbing their teats and pulling event. I don't know why, but the idea kind of grossed me out. However, as fewer men were left to do a greater number of projects, I realized I needed to step in and help.

For a season, I reluctantly got up at 4:30 a.m. and stumbled over to the tabernacle, where I joined my bleary-eyed companions. In the predawn darkness, we shuffled single file down the slippery boardwalks towards the barn, straining to see what lay ahead, blinded by the brilliance of the gas lantern as it swung back and forth with the cadence of the

Wilderness Blues

lead man. The shadows we cast on the muskegs gave the procession an eerie appearance. The distant call of hoot owls lent a Poe-like atmosphere to the scene.

When we opened the barn door, my nostrils were assailed with the warm stench of animal bodies, hay and manure. It was an odd mixture of smells, which clung to your clothes like a baby possum to its mother's back. The scent was so powerful that, during deer-hunting season, some of the more knowledgeable hunters left their wool clothing hanging in the barn. They claimed the animal smell helped to disguise their own scent.

The cows slowly rose to their feet when we entered. Their bags were full, and they were ready to be milked. That's not all that was full. As soon as they stood up, their tails lifted and a stream of urine gushed out. I quickly learned to stand at the front until after the initial flood. Pee wasn't the only thing to watch out for. There was one cow that I absolutely refused to milk. After she relieved her bladder, her tail would raise a few inches and she would fart; not just one or two times (that I could handle) but for a solid five minutes at intervals of about two seconds. On the one hand, I could relate to her; since my move to Mt. Bether, I had become a regular gasbag myself. Everything I ate gave me gas, but this was ridiculous. All four of her stomachs were filled to capacity. Even if I had wanted to milk her, I couldn't because I was laughing too hard. Tears streamed down my face, blurring my vision, and my guts hurt from the convulsions. Now, I don't know what's so funny about an animal's relief – nothing really, I guess – except that it carried on for so long. If there was a Guinness Book of World Records for the passing of gas by bovines, I'm relatively sure she would have made the cut.

One of the milking crew, an elder named James, seemed to be the one who usually milked the fartsack. An older man, sixtyish and balding, he was blessed with the most

Chapter Twenty-Five

beautiful tenor voice. Normally good-natured, he walked around the camp singing or whistling and tackled every task with equal gusto. He was able to see beauty in almost anything. On our way to the barn in the early morning, while I complained about the cold or dark, he'd search out some good thing.

"My God, look at those stars sparkling!" he'd say with excitement in his voice. "I bet it's going to be a gorgeous day."

His childlike excitement could be contagious.

"Just look at the patterns the frost is making on the boardwalk. God is such an artist, isn't he, Tom?" While I was looking, he would express his thanks to a Creator who would take the time to draw a design on a frozen boardwalk for our pleasure.

"Father, what a wonderful thing you've done," he'd say, smiling. Then he would head off to take care of the chore at hand.

Prior to moving to the farm, he had been a professional illustrator for a defense contractor on the East Coast. Now, he spent his days chopping firewood and milking cows, which he did cheerfully. When he entered the barn, he always spoke to the animals.

"Good morning, ladies," he'd say in a New England accent. "How are you all doing today?" Then sauntering over to the cow with the gastric problem, he would address her.

"How are you this morning, Madam Queen?"

I believe the cow's name was Maybell, but he always referred to her as Madam Queen. It runs in my mind that he occasionally addressed some of the ladies around the camp with the same title, but I'm certain no disrespect was intended.

The cow never seemed to pay any attention, apparently content to chew her cud and pollute the air with methane, her tail moving up and down like a kid on a teeter-totter.

Wilderness Blues

Grabbing our stools and buckets, we stationed ourselves under the cows, first brushing and then washing their undersides. Their tails were tied to the stalls to prevent being slapped in the face while we worked. After the preparations were made, we were ready to start milking. Grasping a teat in each hand and with a squeezing, downward tugging motion, we set the milk flowing, splashing in the buckets with a ringing sound. The whole process took about 15 minutes, and when I was done, the muscles in my forearms felt like I had been turning wrenches for hours. If I'd tattooed an anchor on them, I could have competed in a Popeye lookalike contest.

The animal program grew to include chickens and goats, as well as a bull and more horses and pigs. I don't know why we had the pigs. I only recall eating pork once the whole time I lived there, and then it tasted like fish because that's what they had been fed.

Of all the animals we raised, the horses were my least favorite. Though I had run-ins with the cows (they cropped the heads off some dinner plate dahlias that were on the verge of blooming) and with the goats (they ate a lilac bush that I had diligently cared for all spring), it was still the horses that distressed me the most. There was one young stallion named Sunrise who was a real troublemaker. Jan swears that she watched him grasp a stick in his mouth and walk down the side of the greenhouse poking holes in the plastic. He had bitten several of the people who worked with him and had the reputation of being ill tempered. He used to stand out on the mudflats feeding on beach asparagus and threaten anyone walking by. Once, I had to grab a piece of driftwood just to insure safe passage across the flats when he was there. Eventually, we slaughtered and ate him. I guess we had the last bite. What an appropriate way to deal with all your enemies.

There was another horse that troubled me as well. We

Chapter Twenty-Five

were having problems with the animals sneaking into the vegetable gardens, so I was asked to escort them to the pasture one day. I was in a bit of a hurry to do something and Marge, an old mare, was dawdling, so I thought I'd try what the Plains Indians used to do and ride her out bareback. That was a mistake. With a handful of mane, I attempted to mount. As I placed my weight on her, she jumped forward and kicked with both hooves. The pain was indescribable. Though I was happy that my face had been spared, I was unsure whether I would ever take a deep breath again. The horse's aim was uncanny. While I lay on the ground, trying to get some air into my lungs, Dave Ames, who had witnessed the whole thing, sauntered over.

"You gonna be alright there, Brother Tom?" he asked.

I wasn't much in the mood for talking, even if I could have. Then his wife, Danita, rushed up. At 4'11" and thin as a rail, she wasn't much bigger than many of the kids around the camp. She had white, almost translucent skin that stood in stark contrast to her large, brown eyes and coal-black hair. Her voice, when she spoke, was high-pitched, like a young boy's and filled with concern.

"Oh my God, David, what happened?" she asked, wringing her hands.

Calm and deliberate, he answered her. "Brother Tom was kicked in the groin by a horse, honey."

"Oh my, is there anything I can do?"

"I don't think so, honey. I think he'll just have to lie there until he gets his breath back."

The whole scenario was somewhat comical, and if I hadn't been in so much pain, I might have come up with some smart aleck remark. Just as well that I was hurting, I guess. To make matters worse, my oldest daughter, Jennifer, who was about 10 at the time, showed up on the scene – just what I needed, an audience.

Distraught over seeing me lying on the ground, she

Wilderness Blues

started crying.

"Is my dad going to die?" she asked David.

"No," he assured her, "but he probably feels like he is."

After some time had passed, I was able to get up and walk gingerly home, where I spent the rest of the day. Apparently, there was no lasting damage. Some months later, my twin boys were conceived.

Needless to say, I never tried the bareback stunt again, and though what happened may not have been the horse's fault, nonetheless, I didn't shed any tears when she died.

There were a number of goats on the farm. I guess they were pretty easy to raise and would eat just about anything. One of the teenage girls took care of them for the most part, and they would follow her around the camp dutifully. The females that had given birth had such large teats that they would drag along the ground, and occasionally, they would even step on themselves and require stitches. I can only remember one billy goat, which was kept penned up. It was a good thing, too. Any female that passed by would drive him crazy. He would beat the bars of his pen and put his forelegs on the top of the gate in a desperate attempt to get out. As I recall, he stank, too. Fortunately, I never had much reason to go down to the goat barn; they kind of freaked me out.

Old age eventually claimed the oxen. When it became apparent they couldn't pull their share of the load anymore, we slaughtered and ate them. As you can imagine, they were as tough as nails. Adam, the first pig, died when the door on his pen slammed down on his head and killed him. I guess someone forgot to bend over a nail that protruded through the wooden door. I suppose Eve must have found a different significant other. It seems like there were a lot of pigs when we left the farm. It runs in my mind that most of the chickens were slaughtered, though I don't know why. I was surprised to see that they really do run around crazy when

Chapter Twenty-Five

their heads are chopped off. I think the bulls were eliminated, also – too dangerous to have with so many little kids around. I don't know whatever happened to Maybell. I can only assume that she went to cow heaven, where she is probably responsible for at least some of the clouds that float by.

Chapter Twenty-Six

On more than one occasion, while at the weekly meetings or sitting down to dinner with the rest of the congregation, I would take a glance at the people I was surrounded by. There were very few that I knew well and even less that I would call my friends. At such times, when I allowed myself to go there, I wondered, what the hell am I doing here? I don't belong here! Who are these people?

It was a question worth asking. Do normal people pack up their belongings and move thousands of miles away from family and friends to take on the lifestyle of their ancestors? I always considered my upbringing fairly normal. There was nothing in the way I was raised that would propel me into such an unorthodox existence. What had I been thinking?

If my fellow farmers had been unsavory characters or shown signs of mental instability, no doubt I would have had an easier time pegging them as losers, but the fact was, this diverse group was average in almost every way, except for their unwavering commitment to the farm. People who had been teachers, musicians, construction foremen, architects, engineers, truck drivers, homemakers and even a baby food salesman surrounded me. Of course, there were a few screwballs in the group, just like any gathering of people, and I had a hard time with some of the personalities, but by and large, they were pretty average. The fact that they appeared so ordinary and had lived successful lives prior to moving to the farm made it hard for me to believe that they could all be wrong about moving here. I just didn't share the same zeal that they seemed to have for this way of life.

No one at the camp was more distant from me ideologically than Brother Jerry. Jerry Horowitz, a short, wiry, balding man, had been born into a Jewish family and was now living on a Christian farm. Prior to getting involved with the

Chapter Twenty-Six

Move, he had lived a rather worldly lifestyle, a fact that he now regretted. He had been involved in advertising and had worked at one time with a famous television producer. He didn't like to say much about his past, preferring to concentrate on his new life, which he pursued with a vengeance.

In matters relating to the farm, we couldn't have been more different. While I despised being there and spent most of my early years complaining about all things pertaining to the place, Jerry loved it and would frequently bring guests out to visit.

I felt as if storm clouds encircled my head and spent my days moping about the camp. In stark contrast, he strutted around as if he had just won the lottery, singing and smiling; he was in heaven itself. Though I tried to avoid him as much as I could, encounters were inevitable. Whenever we met, the scenario was always the same.

"Thomas!" It was a declaration like "Eureka!" "How are you doing, Brother?" he would ask sincerely.

"Lousy," I'd mumble. He always looked at me like he was in a state of disbelief when I answered. I think it caught him off guard that anyone could be having a less than stellar day on the farm.

"Well, I'm sorry to hear that, Brother Tom. It sounds like you're going through the fire. If you'd like, we could pray right now."

"No thanks, Jerry. I've got some other stuff I've got to go do."

"Okay then. Have a good day. I'll be thinking about you."

"Yeah, thanks, Jerry."

"One more thing, Thomas."

"Yeah, Jerry, what's that?"

"God loves you, Brother."

"Yeah, okay, Jerry. I'll try to remember that."

And so it would go. He was a very nice guy, and some

Wilderness Blues

years later, we would become friends, but at the time, he was way too zealous for me to relate to. I wasn't the only one who had a hard time with him. His religious zeal irritated both Uncle Bill and Tim and a few of the other fellows, too, primarily the men who worked in town. He was frequently the topic of conversation, providing us with more than a few entertaining stories. His fervor to perform whatever task was at hand landed him in more than a few difficult if not dangerous positions.

Jerry had a love affair with boats, though as far as I know, he had never owned one prior to moving to Alaska. To the best of my knowledge, his first boat was an abandoned derelict named the *Diver,* an old wooden troller that had been left to pound against the pilings at the side of the cold storage. I had just assumed it would meet the fate of so many wooden boats in this cold, wet climate and fall apart from neglect. However, Jerry had other plans.

He somehow managed to float the old gal to the farm where he could work on it, which he did, day after day. Many of the men felt like this was a waste of time, that there were other projects more pressing – like chopping firewood or removing snow from the boardwalks. However, Jerry somehow prevailed with his project and even managed to get someone to help him get the engine running, more or less. It was a source of great joy for him, and he even decided to change the name of the boat to the *Pearl,* as in a pearl of great price, in reference to a scripture from the Bible.

Jerry decided to put the boat to work and purchased a salmon troll, as well as a halibut license. The fact that he had no experience didn't deter him in the least.

"Family," he announced one night at dinner, "I'm going to speak the word of faith and believe that God would have me put the *Pearl* to work in the fishing industry. With the help of the brethren, she's finally ready for her maiden voy-

Chapter Twenty-Six

age." Waving his hands and smiling broadly, he continued on. "Tomorrow I will take her out and test the waters. I would greatly covet your prayers."

Nothing further needed to be said. Fervent prayers were immediately dispatched heavenward. However, whether the prayers were on Jerry's behalf or for anyone who may cross his path, I wasn't sure.

Halibut season arrived, and Jerry decided to give it a go. He scrounged up a few skates of gear and made arrangements for one of the young men from the farm to go with him as his crew hand. He chose a strapping young fellow named Eric who had a pleasant attitude and a good sense of humor, a necessary attribute. As far as I know, it was his first and last trip with Brother Jerry, but it was to be a memorable one.

I can't remember all the particulars of that first voyage. It was inconceivable that everything would go without a hitch, that's just part of having a boat, no matter who you are. Given the fact that the boat was salvaged from the beach and put together with spare parts scrounged from around the camp, problems were inevitable.

According to Eric, they got the long line gear baited and set out without too much difficulty. After it had soaked for a reasonable length of time, they decided to pull the gear and see if they had caught any halibut. That's when the problems started.

"Somehow we managed to run over the line while we were pulling gear," Eric laughed. "He stood on the deck and looked down into the water where the line was. You could see that it was running right back into the prop. I didn't know what to do. I figured we'd have to wait for someone to come rescue us, but Jerry had a plan."

As he proceeded to tell me the story, he kept laughing harder, until I could hardly understand what it was he was saying.

Wilderness Blues

"There were some 40-pound cannonballs on the deck that Jerry had tied some lines to. Then he went into the cabin and put on his survival suit. 'I'm going to go down below,' he said, 'and see if I can free the line. You stay here and hang onto the rope that's tied around my waist.' So that's what I did. Of course, as soon as he jumped into the water, he floated like a cork.

"'Eric,' he said, 'pass me down one of the cannonballs.' He tied it to one of his legs, and when he did, one leg was down and the other was still floating on the surface. 'Give me the other cannonball, Brother.' So I passed him the other one. When he tied it on, he sank out of sight. I looked over the stern of the boat, and I could see him looking up at me as he was sinking. Fortunately, I had hold of the line that was tied to his waist and was able to hoist him up.

"'I think that's too much weight, Brother. Let's try the 25-pound leads.' So we switched them. They offset the buoyancy of the suit enough to allow him to work on the hull. He put a knife in his mouth like a pirate and went under the boat to cut the line. I could hear him down below sawing the rope, and every minute or so, he came to the surface for air. At one point, he came up with his tongue sticking out and his face streaked with red bottom paint. 'I thug I wos a flig,' he jabbered. I stared at him for a few seconds, confused. Finally, I realized he wanted me to take something off his tongue. 'Eric, I think I lost a filling.' I looked at what was in my hand. It was a barnacle. I was laughing so hard, I almost lost my grip on the line."

This story made its way around the camp and even into Hoonah. It was just one of many mishaps that involved Brother Jerry. In a scary sort of way, he was famous.

It runs in my mind that the resurrection of the *Diver* was short lived. I think there were just too many problems to justify keeping it, and I believe it ended up on the backside of Graveyard Island, a fitting end to a fine old boat.

Chapter Twenty-Six

Like I said, Jerry had a love affair with boats, so when the *Diver* found its final resting place, he replaced it with another, this time a skiff. It was on this skiff that another well talked about incident occurred.

Brother Jerry was a very charismatic fellow and greeted friend and stranger alike with enthusiasm. It was this trait that was the cause for some embarrassment one summer day. As the story goes, he was taking some young people from the farm into town for a sing-along at one of the local churches. It was sunny and warm, a great day to be out on the water. After he loaded the teens into his skiff, he took off for Hoonah. Partway to his destination, he spotted a couple of kayakers out in the bay. Being the friendly fellow he was, he decided to detour and say hi. As they approached the two crafts, it was obvious that both parties were naked from the waist up, apparently trying to take advantage of the infrequent sunshine. Jerry was just raising his hand in a friendly greeting when he realized that one of the two was a woman. Turning abruptly away, he sped off for his original destination, admonishing his young passengers to not look back.

From day to day, you never knew when the next story would surface. One time, as I rounded the bend on my way out to the farm, I looked towards the beach where we offloaded passengers and freight, and I noticed a boat sitting high and dry on a large rock, perfectly balanced, like it belonged there. As I approached, I heard a familiar salutation.

"Thomas! Yo, Brother!"

"Jerry, what the heck are you doing there? How did that happen?"

With much hand waving and pointing, he explained, "Well, I was offloading some passengers onto the beach, and I guess I misjudged the tide. When is high water?"

I told him, and we decided that he should stay with the boat until it could float again. I went into the camp, amazed

Wilderness Blues

that the boat had set down on that uneven, barnacle-encrusted rock so nicely.

Not all of his adventures ended so well, though. I was working on the fuel dock at Kane's one summer day, when Jerry pulled up for gas. I wasn't especially happy to see him; like I said, he just rubbed me the wrong way. He was a customer though, and since there was no one else around to pump him the fuel, I passed down the hose. When he was all done, I did the paperwork and went into the cold storage to see if any big loads of fish had been brought in. While I was in a conversation with one of the workers, I heard someone scream, "FIRE!"

Rushing through the door, I shouted, "Where?"

"The fuel dock!" came the reply.

As I came around the corner, I could see the shimmering waves of heat rising from below. Seconds later, flames topped the bull rail that encircled the dock. In a panic, I rushed towards the edge, getting as close as the heat would allow, praying, begging for God's mercy, even as I envisioned the worst. There was no way anyone could survive that inferno. The blaze was towering above the dock, threatening to engulf the creosote pilings of the structure. People were rushing to the edge, discharging fire extinguishers, trying to knock down the awful flames. Shaking with dread, I shouted down below.

"Jerry!"

I was expecting no response.

What I got was the unmistakable voice of one of the most optimistic, confident, God loving and irritating people I had ever met.

"It's all right, Tom! I'm okay."

"Jerry, where are you at?"

"I'm down here, hanging onto the ladder."

A hundred thoughts passed through my mind at lightning speed. My sense of relief at his safety was tempered by

Chapter Twenty-Six

the vision of the entire town burning down again. (It was destroyed by fire in 1944.)

"Can you untie the boat?"

"Yes!" he called back. "Yes, I think I can reach the rope!"

Seconds later, and none too soon, the skiff started drifting away from the dock, still burning.

Much to my surprise, there was no explosion. The boat burned all the way down to the waterline and ended up on Graveyard Island that evening. The next day, the tide lifted it off, and it ended up drifting around Icy Straits for a week, where the Coast Guard declared it a hazard to navigation.

Jerry climbed up the ladder about the same time that the volunteer fire department showed up. He was drenched and left little puddles of water on the planking as he sauntered down the dock, shaking the hands of well-wishers and searching for his wife in the crowd.

I talked to him later, after he'd changed into dry clothes and had a chance to gather his thoughts.

"Jerry, what the heck happened? How did the fire start?"

"Well," he said with some flourish, "I had been having problems with the carburetor not getting any fuel, so I ran a hose from a five-gallon can to it while I filled the main tanks. I guess the hose fell out and filled up the bilge with gasoline. The switch that I turn on the bilge pump with was broken, so I had to connect the wires from the switch to the battery in the back. When I did, it arched and set the boat on fire."

I was at a loss for words, so I shook my head and left, marveling at the way he had escaped, unharmed.

While he still wasn't on my top 10 favorite people list, after that day, my attitude towards Brother Jerry changed. I think the idea that he might have died in that inferno made me stop and consider our relationship. While we weren't the best of friends, and he still aggravated the huss out of me on

Wilderness Blues

occasion, he was nonetheless a part of my life, and I needed to respect him.

That being said, I often wondered: Considering all the accidents he seemed prone to, was the Lord irritated with him, or did he love him so much that he kept a special watch on him? I'm going to assume it's the latter.

Chapter Twenty-Seven

I've always enjoyed fishing a lot. When the eldership in Charleston started talking about moving to Alaska, it was the idea of fishing that appealed to me, not the end of the world talk or the moving on into perfection stuff. Alaska was a place fishermen dreamed of. When I first moved to Game Creek, the fishing was the one thing I wasn't disappointed in. Standing on the creek bank, it wasn't unusual to catch a Dolly Varden trout on every cast. There were so many fish that if you hooked one and it got off, frequently, another would strike before your lure reached the shore. It was a lot of fun and gave me something to look forward to on many summer days.

One day in late winter, Bob Cramer approached me about being a crew hand on his boat. Though I had a hand troll license for salmon, I had never fished for halibut before, which is what Bob was going after. I had quit working in town to build our home, and with that out of the way, it left me free to pursue the fishing. This was a good chance to make a few bucks and do something besides chop wood for a while, which suited me fine.

It was only February, but Bob was already making preparations for the upcoming season in May. "Come on over to the house, Tom, and I'll show you how to tie gangions," he said.

"What the heck are gangions?" I asked, as we walked towards his cabin.

"Short pieces of heavy nylon line used for leaders," he said. "I like size 72 (referring to the thickness of the line). It's strong enough to catch the big females and holds up well on a rocky bottom."

When we got to the cabin, he brought out several bundles of gangions. Each bundle held 100 of the abrasive, stiff

Wilderness Blues

white lines. They were about 42 inches long and made of braided nylon. I'd never fished with anything but monofilament before and couldn't see how such heavy gear could be effective. If the leaders were this big, how large were the hooks that fit on them and what kind of fish would be fooled by such heavy gear?

It was unseasonably warm that day, so we decided to enjoy the rare sunshine. We stepped out on the front porch, and Bob grabbed a couple chairs. He sat in one and turned the other over.

"Watch," he commanded, and took a gangion from the bundle. "First, you wrap the end around the chair leg to form a loop. Then push the small end over the longer end with your index finger and wrap the long end around and through. Pull it tight, and you're done. The harder the fish pull, the tighter it gets."

He held up the gangion for inspection. It had a loop in the end, but for what purpose I had no idea.

"Make sure you make the loop large enough to go over the shank of the hook. Each gangion needs at least one large loop. The other end can be smaller."

It wasn't until he produced a box of 16/0 hooks and a package of line snaps that any of this made sense. I took a hook in my hand and inspected it. It was larger than anything I had ever seen. "Man, look at the size of this hook," I muttered.

"It takes a big hook to catch a big fish," he smiled. "You should see the hunk of bait we use." Then turning to the task at hand, he tied the other end of the line. "Why don't you go ahead and try tying some. As soon as you're sure you've got it, I'll have to leave. Sam needs some help with the tractor."

Bob was an excellent teacher, patient and knowledgeable, and after a few tries, I got the hang of tying the leaders.

Chapter Twenty-Seven

"Here," he said, "you might need this." He handed me a roll of black electrical tape. "We've got 19 more bundles to tie and your fingers are going to get sore if you don't tape them up."

As usual, he knew what he was talking about. By the end of the day, I had tied only 300 gangions, and the fingers on my right hand were raw and aching, and the joints were stiffening up like rusty hinges. I half expected them to squeak when I flexed them.

Halfway through the day, Bob stopped by to check on my progress. He stepped out on the porch and offered me a cookie. "Here ya go, Thomas. I don't want you to get weak and pass out on me. Judy and the kids made these up the other day. Try one, they're pretty good."

"Hey, thanks, Bob." I'd been on the farm long enough to know that when food was offered, you didn't hesitate. It might not be offered again.

"How are your fingers holding out?" he asked. "Have your blisters got blisters?"

"Man, I guess," I said between bites. "These gangions are tough on the old skinaroo."

"Just wait. By the time you're all finished tying these, you'll have the hands of a real fisherman."

I smiled and started daydreaming about all the fish I might catch — salmon, halibut, gray cod. I'd already had good luck with a herring gillnet. In fact, I'd plugged it several years in a row and didn't have to buy any bait for trolling. Maybe this was my calling. Maybe I was meant to be a commercial fisherman. My thoughts were interrupted when I heard my name.

"What? What's that, Robert?"

Bob shoved the rest of his cookie into his mouth and reached into the pocket of his coveralls. "Here," he said, producing a small, thin bastard file. "We're going to have to sharpen all the hooks before you put them away."

Wilderness Blues

"Sharpen the hooks? Why do we have to sharpen the hooks? They're all brand new."

Without answering, he reached into the box and drew out a hook. Holding it between his thumb and forefinger, he ran the file over the point several times. "Check this out," he said.

I took it from him and felt the newly sharpened point. The difference was measurable.

"New hooks are seldom as sharp as they should be. They're just stamped out at the factory. You don't want to lose a $100 fish just because of dull hooks."

"Yeah, good point," I muttered, as I started sharpening. I checked every one of those 2,000 hooks for sharpness. If we lost any fish, it wasn't going to be because of me. To keep the 2,000 hooks from tangling with each other, Bob had me separate them into bundles of 50 and cover them with paper bags until we needed them.

Once the gangions were all tied and hooks and snaps attached, there wasn't much more for me to do to prepare for fishing until we got closer to the halibut season. In the meantime, there was still wood to chop and buildings to build and 100 other things that needed done around the camp. Knowing that I was going to be part of the halibut crew made everything seem a little more tolerable.

In early spring, Bob constructed a gridiron for his boat on the mudflats, across from the camp. A gridiron, or grid, was made up of pilings driven into mud or sand, with horizontal beams set across them. The beams were usually elevated a few feet to allow movement beneath them. It was preferable to have the grid on a sloping beach with upright poles or pilings on the beach side sticking above the horizontal beams, providing the boat a place to lean against after the tide went out. Once on the grid, it was easy to paint the keel or replace zincs or do any other work on the boat bottom that needed to be done – short of replacing planks or

Chapter Twenty-Seven

ribs, something that might require being hauled out of the water altogether.

As part of the fishing crew, I was assigned to help paint the bottom of the *Miss Valerie*, Bob's boat. The paint we used was specially formulated to prevent the growth of marine algae and to act as a deterrent to wood-eating pests, like torrido worms. I was surprised to see how heavy it was – much heavier than a gallon of regular house paint – probably from all the cuprous oxide inside.

Once the tide receded, we had to work fast to scrub the bottom and remove the old zincs. With any luck, the sun would appear, or a little breeze would come up to speed the drying process. Bob was busy poking at the seams with a putty knife. Any loose cement was reefed out and replaced. There was only a short window between tides to complete our task. As the saying goes, time and tide wait for no man. In the few hours that we had on the grid, we accomplished a marathon number of chores in record time. As the tide started to creep onto the mudflats, we gathered up empty paint cans and scrub brushes and headed back to the camp. I turned around to look at the *Miss Valerie*. She had the classic lines of a wooden troller. Sitting on the grid, she really looked sharp. The fresh coat of bottom paint stood out nicely against the crisp white of the hull. She was a good-looking, seaworthy boat, and I was looking forward to fishing on her.

As the season approached, there was a new round of activity. Flags were made for bamboo poles. Different colors of cloth were used to help us distinguish our gear from the other boats that would be fishing the same area. The flags, when tethered to a floating buoy, marked each end of our lines as they soaked on the ocean bottom. We loaded a skiff with all the gangions, anchors and flagpoles and other things that Bob felt would be useful and took it all to the *Miss Valerie*, which was anchored out at the point.

Wilderness Blues

On the morning of the opening, we were up early. Several of the ladies had spent the previous few days cooking for the halibut crew, and we were loaded to the gills with chow and not the usual stuff that we were used to eating, either. There wasn't a rutabaga or turnip in the whole batch. No siree, we had jello with fruit, lunchmeat sandwiches, some biscuits with egg and cheese and 20 dozen chocolate chip cookies. That's just part of what I remember. I had never eaten like this on the farm before. There were four men in the crew, including Bob. We were going to be gone for five days, but even so, I didn't think we could possibly eat all that food. I was wrong. We ate two dozen cookies before we ever left Hoonah.

We stopped in town to pick up some bait at the cold storage. Bob liked using octopus, even though it was more expensive than herring or gray cod. After a quick lesson in baiting the hooks, we took off. We were headed to Point Adolphus, a natural gathering place for halibut coming into Icy Straits from the ocean. Several other boats were ahead of us, leaving a wake behind them. Though we had gotten up early to go to town, by the time we picked up bait and ice, we were one of the last boats to leave the dock. It was already 8:00 a.m., and Adolphus was a three-hour run. The halibut opening started at noon. It was going to be close.

With the hold full of ice and a long-line reel filled to capacity, the *Miss Valerie* was setting pretty low in the water. With the added weight of anchors, bait, buoys and flagpoles, I wasn't sure where we would put any fish. Up in the focsile, where the sleeping quarters were, there wasn't much room, either. All the extra clothes for four men were piled up there, plus sleeping bags and dry food stores. For the next few days, eating, sleeping and getting up to take a leak would resemble a Chinese fire drill. Any shifting of bodies required the cooperation of the whole group. For some reason though, it didn't seem to bother us. We were off the farm

Chapter Twenty-Seven

and working together, and there was a sense of camaraderie amongst us that was refreshing.

Bob steered the boat from inside the cabin while my fellow crewmembers helped bait hooks in the stern cockpit with me.

I was happy to be with the other two guys; both were pretty laid back and not too religious. Sam Selkirk was the oldest of the three. Though he was only in his 30s, he looked quite a bit older. He was getting gray and there were lines in his face and forehead. His liquid blue eyes held a hint of sadness, and when he laughed, which wasn't often, it seemed insincere, almost as if he were afraid to be happy. He was quiet most of the time, but he worked hard and could figure out anything mechanical, which was a real asset on a boat.

Mark Rawlins was the other crew hand. Just out of his teens, he was tall and strong – a good-looking kid with straight dark hair and an easy smile. He liked to joke around and laughed at almost anything I said. We talked and laughed as we baited each hook and draped them over the stern.

The octopus we were using had a unique smell. It didn't smell fishy, but you could tell it had definitely come from the sea. I had never even seen an octopus before, except on TV, so it was a new experience for me. We cut the arms into lengths large enough to cover each hook completely, with some to spare. The suckers that covered each arm were like suction cups, and though they had been just recently removed from the blast freezer, on occasion, they stuck to the surface of the cutting boards and made a loud popping sound when we pulled them loose. I preferred to bait the tentacles, as they were more solid than the fleshy, slippery head. I can only liken it to shoving a hook into a block of jello. Bob liked using octopus because it stayed on the hook well and kept fishing, unlike herring, which was soft and

Wilderness Blues

would wash away after a few hours in the tide. Frequently, we caught fish and were able to reuse the octopus. Pound for pound, it was some of the best bait you could use.

We baited hooks all the way out to the fishing grounds. As we approached Point Adolphus, the water became more turbulent. Strong currents pulled at the boat, and islands of kelp formed in the tiderips, swirling, breaking apart and re-forming. Hundreds of herring gulls and arctic terns squawked and dived on the feed that was pushed to the surface. There was quite a large gathering of humpback whales, too. Six or eight were visible at any one time, spouting and gliding effortlessly, their black bodies glistening in the daylight. As we got closer to them, I noticed that all of them seemed to have clusters of barnacles growing on their heads, not unlike the bottom of the boat.

We continued west, past the blinker, and 20 minutes later were in calmer water. When I looked up again, we were surrounded by boats – dozens of boats, of every size and shape imaginable. I had no idea that the halibut season would attract such a large, diverse group, but with few restrictions, anyone with a boat and a halibut license could participate and did. Everything from schooners to skiffs showed up. There were trollers and seiners and gillnetters and some boats that I didn't know what they were. There were bow pickers and stern pickers and boats that pulled their gear from the side.

As we passed by them, we read the names – *Kipling*, *Fireweed*, *Miss Jennifer* and the *Sockeye King*. I checked the home ports listed on the stern of each boat – Hoonah, Haines, Juneau, Gustavus, Pelican and even a few from much farther away like Seattle and Port Townsend.

Though the area we were fishing in was relatively large, maybe five miles wide and 10 miles long, there were so many boats that it was hard to find a place that wasn't already occupied. We ran to a spot about a mile off the beach,

Chapter Twenty-Seven

midway between Mud Bay and Point Adolphus and put the boat in neutral. It was almost noon, and we ran inside to get a sandwich before the excitement began. Mark and I were sitting on the hatch cover, eating, when we noticed a small, white gillnetter cruising towards us full tilt, with gray-white smoke billowing out of its exhaust. As it got closer, we could read the name on the bow – the *Mayo*. It was almost upon us before the captain slowed her down and pulled up alongside, leaving both boats bouncing in his wake. The crews were sizing each other up when Bob came out of the cabin.

A short, dark-haired native fellow stepped out onto the deck of the other boat and called over to Bob. "You the captain?"

"Yeah," Bob answered, "what do you need?"

"Where are you planning on setting your gear? I've been sitting on this spot for two hours, ya know, and I don't appreciate you coming in and trying to set down in front of me."

"I passed you a half mile back. I don't know how much gear you're running, but I think we can stay out of each other's way." Bob wasn't easily intimidated.

"Yeah, well, I don't think it's right that you should just come in here like that. Whoever gets here first is supposed to get the spot. Are you setting with the tide?"

Bob assured him he was, and that seemed to pacify the other captain, who left in a puff of smoke and returned to his previous station. For the rest of the trip, we made smart aleck comments about fictitious boats named after various condiments trying to contact the *Mayo* (the *Mayo*, the *Mayo* ... the *Mustard Jar* calling). It was goofy, but it gave us something to laugh about when we were tired.

The VHF radio in the cabin was tuned to channel 16, and there was a steady stream of chatter coming over the airwaves. At noon, word went out that the halibut opening

Wilderness Blues

had officially started. Immediately, every boat in the fleet tossed out buoys and flags and the madness began. Sam and Mark stood in the cockpit, first tossing a 40-pound anchor into the water, then snapping baited hooks onto the line that was peeling off the large hydraulic reel mounted in the stern. Hooks were attached about every 15 to 18 feet, or more frequently if we were over a good spot, something only the captain could determine. Bob stayed in the cabin, steering and watching the depth of the water on a fathometer as we moved forward with the current. Periodically, he would call out the door, "Put on a cannonball here, we're going over a deep hole." After he felt like enough line was laid down, we would stop, attach an anchor, buoy and flagpole and go to make another set.

The long-line reel, or drum, on the *Miss Valerie* had 20 skates of quarter-inch, tarred nylon line. Each skate was 1,800 feet long, so by the time we had laid it all out, there was several miles of ocean bottom covered with baited hooks — and that was just our boat.

We made five sets of various lengths and pulled over to a shallow cove to anchor and give the bait time to soak. It had taken several hours to set all the gear, and Bob thought it would be best if we didn't pick the sets until the next morning, after the tides had gone through a complete cycle of highs and lows. In the meantime, we broke out the chow and ate.

I heard a noise and looked behind the boat. A dark form swam effortlessly through the water and surfaced again, blowing and sucking in air. A whiskered face looked up at me before disappearing into the deep. It was a large sea lion. Point Adolphus is a natural gathering place for them. All the feed attracts salmon, cod and herring and other fish that the sea lions feed on. While they were fun to watch while at anchor, they were cursed by most salmon trollers because of their habit of following boats and taking fish off the hooks.

Chapter Twenty-Seven

They were seldom satisfied eating just one or two and would frequently stay behind one boat until the fisherman was forced to pull his gear and leave the area or pull up close to another troller and try to pass the nuisance off to them.

There wasn't much to do while we waited. Bob sat in the captain's chair and poured over a chart of the area, checking to see the makeup of the bottom, whether it was rocky or sandy, if it had any drop offs or high spots and where the currents were likely to push the fish. He had mapped out the area where we set the gear and checked the tide book to see what the current would be doing in the morning so he knew which end of the set to start pulling first. The rest of us just talked or listened to the VHF. Once in a while, someone would call another boat and direct them to a working channel. Of course, we had to tune in since it was our only source of entertainment.

"*Santa Rosa*, if you get any closer, I'm going to climb in your mast and shit in your hair."

There was silence and then, "Woo, Woo!" A few seconds passed before someone else piped in, "Well…alrighty then."

Without fail, there was always someone who would start carrying on a conversation on channel 16, the hailing and distress channel. Then the Coast Guard would have to come on and tell them to go to a working channel, but usually not before several of the more experienced users swore at them for being so stupid.

We also heard people cursing other boats for setting lines on top of their sets and various other infractions. There was a good bit of tension in the air, as you would expect any time a large group of people is vying for the same resource.

Berthing was limited on the *Miss Valerie*, but with one fellow on the floor, one on the bench and two in a double berth up front, we all managed to find a place to sleep. The

Wilderness Blues

next day, after breakfast, we weighed the anchor and went to pick our first set. We used different colored buoys with matching flags to make our sets easier to identify in the sea of orange or pink fluorescent buoys that were scattered around the area. Though each buoy was required to have the boat name and Department of Fish and Game number on it, if you weren't paying attention when you set your gear, it could be difficult to find later. To make matters worse, tugboats towing barges regularly passed through the area, sometimes snagging gear and towing it far from where it was set. Sometimes it could be retrieved, often times it was lost for good, along with any fish that may have been hooked. With the introduction of individual fishing quotas and the months long seasons, halibut fishermen aren't forced to fish all together at the same time, so the chance of losing gear isn't quite as great. However, with the tremendous increase in cruise ship traffic, losing gear to large ships may become a problem again.

As we ran towards our first set, I was amazed at the number of buoys that were scattered about. The bright floats bouncing in the current reminded me of an Easter egg hunt. Other boats were already pulling their gear, and I watched with fascination as lines came over the side with fish swinging from gangions and were either pulled aboard or shaken off and returned to the water. The legal size for halibut is 32 inches; anything smaller had to be released. While we were heading to our set, we all donned our rain gear, rubber boots and gloves. Fishing is wet work, even on sunny days.

Bob maneuvered the boat alongside our first buoy and flag, and we grabbed it and pulled it aboard. We untied them and retied the ground line to the reel. Bob climbed into the cockpit and took control. He was a one man fishing machine – steering the boat, running the hydraulics, keeping the line straight on the reel and stunning the fish. He was totally

Chapter Twenty-Seven

immersed in what he was doing and, at the same time, aware of every other aspect of the operation. If someone was doing something dangerous, he was aware of it and corrected him. I had complete confidence in his ability to get us home safely.

My job was to stay in the back and take the hooks from Bob that were either empty or had fish other than legal-sized halibut on them. There were a lot of sculpins, or bullheads, in the rocky areas that we fished, as well as the occasional gray cod. I had to remove them and toss them aside for use as bait later. From my station in the stern, I could see the line as it came up from the bottom and watch what each hook yielded. You never knew what was going to be on the next hook – it was always a surprise. On more than one occasion, a bright orange octopus came up on the gear.

It was tossed onto the deck with the intention of using it for bait later, but while we were all occupied, it slunk across the deck and squeezed effortlessly through the small scuppers. Because they have no bones, they can go through exceptionally tight areas. Sometimes we caught 20-legged sun stars, with their multitudes of suction feet grasping the air for something to cling to. Often the line was covered in the delicate brown bodies of basket stars, looking like living doilies, their many tree branch-like arms moving independently. They could have starred in a science fiction movie. Now and then we brought up a skate from a stretch of muddy bottom. They looked similar to the rays that are found in warmer waters. They put up no fight, just hung on the hook like dead weight, which actually made them harder to shake off the hooks. Though they are supposed to be good to eat, there was no market for them, so we shook all that we caught.

When a legal halibut was caught, Bob would grab the gangion, stun the fish with a baseball bat and whistle for Mark to take it. Mark took the line, gaffed the fish and

Wilderness Blues

swung it aboard, making sure that it lay on its back, white side up, before plunging a sharp knife into its gills. Every fish had to be stunned and bled to insure a quality product. We didn't want them flapping around on the deck, bruising the flesh, although most of the fish required repeated blows to the head before they stopped thrashing. The deck was slippery with slime and blood as the day progressed. Halibut covered the area like a lumpy white carpet with more coming aboard all the time. There were stretches of area where they were hanging on the line like sheets on laundry day, one right after another. It was incredibly exciting, but exhausting, too.

Bob kept a .22caliber pistol in a detergent bottle that he had modified to serve as a holster. A leather holster would have gotten ruined in the saltwater environment. When a really big fish was coming up on the line, he whistled for Mark to give him a shark hook, a giant hook attached to a length of ground line which could be tied off to the rail. It was an extra safety precaution against losing the big halibut. When the fish first surfaced, Bob took careful aim and shot it in the head. Then a shark hook was put in its mouth, and it was passed over to Mark. Usually, Sam or I or both of us helped gaff the fish and bring it aboard. Even with a bullet in its brain, these big fish could do some serious damage to the boat and the crew, so we always whacked them a few more times in the head with a bat. Even so, it wasn't uncommon for one of these large females to unexpectedly start thrashing 30 minutes after they were hauled aboard.

A couple times it was apparent that the long-line reel was having trouble pulling the gear. At times, it was because the line was wrapped around an immovable object on the bottom. Once in a while, it was because another boat had set their gear on top of ours. When that happened, Bob put the hydraulic motor in low gear and started pulling up both lines. There was a lot of tension on the line, so a chain puller

Chapter Twenty-Seven

was used to hold the line together while Bob cut the offender's gear. Unlike some people, who would just cut the other guy's gear and let them possibly lose it, Bob always tied their line back together, but not before he slid a damaged rubber glove or a bullhead carcass onto the line, just so they knew they had messed up.

After each set was pulled, we filleted the bullheads and gray cod and used them to bait the hooks so we could reset the gear and keep fishing. We fished from early in the morning until late in the evening, grabbing a bite to eat whenever there was a break and collapsing in our beds at the end of the day. It was a struggle each day to put on our cold, damp raingear. It was hanging outside and felt clammy. Though we all started this trip with three or four pairs of new rubber gloves, by the last day, there wasn't a dry pair to be found. They had all been cut or poked by knives, gaffs or fish teeth. We were all stiff and sore from pulling, cleaning and icing the big fish and fatigue was setting into our bodies.

By the fifth day, we were ready to call it a trip.

For the remainder of the years that I lived on the farm, I fished for halibut with Bob on the *Miss Valerie*. We watched the season go from the original five-day openings to three days, two days and finally, 24-hour derbies. On one three-day opening, we caught an incredible 22,000 pounds and had to go to the scow several times to sell fish. We loaded the boat the first day with 10,000 pounds, and after the fish hold was filled, and there was no more room on the deck, we started hanging the fish over the side of the boat. It was quite an impressive sight. In fact, Bob climbed the mast to get a picture, which he submitted to the *National Fisherman* magazine and ended up winning second place.

I learned a lot while out fishing with Bob Cramer. He is a man of great wisdom and integrity. I was crushed when he told me I couldn't join his crew after we moved off the farm, but in retrospect, it was the best thing that could have

Wilderness Blues

happened. I fish my own boat for halibut now and use the wisdom I learned from my earlier days on the *Miss Valerie*.

I still see Bob in town now and then, and true to his nature, he's always glad to share his knowledge or lend a hand. While we don't see eye to eye on matters relating to the farm, I'm pleased to be able to call him my friend.

Chapter Twenty-Eight

When we moved into the house I'd built, we had five children, all girls. There was Jennifer, Liz, Amber, Camille and Autumn. It was quite a handful, but they were sweet little gals and seemed fairly happy. I had entertained the idea of getting a vasectomy, but before I could get around to it, Jan got pregnant again. I can't help but believe that it was divine providence. On July 31, 1983, my oldest son, Ben, was born. I was in the birthing room with Jan when she delivered him. I was ecstatic! Then the doctor announced that there was a problem. The placenta wasn't coming out. He poked and prodded and then exclaimed, "There's another one in there!"

How could this be? None of the previous doctor visits had indicated that there might be twins. It didn't even show up on the ultrasound. This was 1983, for crying out loud. How can you not know that we're having twins? I didn't know how that was possible, but it was. Brian was a complete surprise. Jan said later that she'd prayed that if she was having a boy, that he would have a brother. She was afraid that one boy with five older sisters would either turn out to be a bully or a wimp.

After a bit, without delivering the second baby, the doctor determined that there was a complication. The baby had the umbilical cord around his neck. They rushed Jan down to surgery to deliver the baby by cesarean section. I stayed behind and signed the papers for the emergency operation. As it was, we ended up with two healthy baby boys.

It just so happened that the operation took place after midnight, so my twin boys have two different birthdays – Ben was born on July 31st, and Brian was born on August 1st. One was born natural and the other C-section. It was a most blessed surprise and a unique event.

Wilderness Blues

While the doctor had Jan open, we decided to put an end to our fertility. We had been so fruitful that the surgeon not only cut the tubes, she tied them and burned the ends. Any future children would be an absolute miracle. Still, even with that in mind, we spent the next year fearful that our ever-expanding family would continue to grow.

After a week or two, we left Juneau and returned to the farm with the boys. When we walked into the tabernacle, the whole congregation was there. High on the wall next to the kitchen, stretching from one side to the other, was an enormous banner welcoming us home. James Doyle, the elder who was an artist, had done the lettering, and it was a sight to behold. Someone had baked a cake, and there was punch and even a skit complete with a song about the boys.

Jan was given time off the women's work schedule so she could take care of the kids. Autumn was still a toddler and needed her attention. One of the young gals volunteered to help Jan with the little ones. In fact, when her family moved off the farm, she stayed with us for a few months to help out. She was like one of our own, and we loved her and still do.

Apparently, someone at the hospital contacted the folks at Ross laboratories, who in turn, sent out a year's supply of powdered baby formula with instructions that there was more available when that was gone. They even paid the freight to get it to us. It was an incredibly generous offer, and we felt truly blessed to receive it.

With three children in diapers, Jan had her hands full. Her mom bought us a ringer washing machine so it wouldn't be necessary to haul dirty clothes to the laundry house, about three blocks away. We kept a 30-gallon garbage can on the porch to collect rainwater for laundry days, but I still had to pack many a five-gallon bucket from the slough out front. Eventually, the water line ran all the way to our house, but we had problems with it freezing in the winter, so most

Chapter Twenty-Eight

laundry days found me struggling up the hill, trying to meet the need for fresh water.

With seven children to be responsible for, I wasn't sure I'd ever be able to leave the farm. I wasn't angry so much, like I had been in the earlier years, but there were still plenty of things that irritated me. We had one of the nicer cabins, and even though there were plenty of inconveniences, we were a lot more comfortable than we used to be. It wasn't a bad life. The kids were safe. They were getting a surprisingly good education. The food was getting better, and things overall were improving. However, I was getting older. I was 32 and had no job, no career and not even a plan for the years ahead. At my age, most men were well entrenched in their vocations, learning and earning and climbing the ladder to success. What did I have?

I had a beautiful wife and seven great kids, but what about our future? I had no car or job or savings. There was no retirement plan waiting for me in my old age, and our house would be worth nothing to us when we left. I didn't want to spend the rest of my days chopping firewood and digging potatoes. I shared my thoughts with Jan, who seemed to be more receptive to leaving than before. I felt like I needed to make a move soon or be on the farm the rest of my life, something I couldn't imagine. I struggled with my thoughts daily, playing the different scenarios over and over in my mind. I prayed and worried and agonized for several more years before we finally committed to leaving.

When we finally decided to make the move, I called my folks to let them know our decision. My dad, who was convinced that we were involved in a cult at one time, wrote me a letter; I believe it was the first one I ever received from him. He tried to discourage me from taking off, knowing full well that we were leaving behind a home and three meals a day and charging off into the unknown. We had no home to go to, no career and not much savings. He knew

Wilderness Blues

full well how hard it is to start over, and I think he was afraid we'd end up out on the street or something. I had the same thoughts coursing through my mind on a daily basis. I was scared to death of making the wrong choice, but if we didn't act now, I'd forever wonder what might have been.

In the winter of 1986, I mentioned to the eldership that we would like to meet with them. The meeting was held upstairs in the schoolhouse. It was one of the bigger cabins and was located right in the center of the camp. It had belonged to the Boryslaws who built it after their place burned down. They moved to another farm in Haines, a town in the northern end of the panhandle. By the time they left, there was no need for additional housing, so their home was requisitioned for the school.

There's not a lot about that gathering that I remember. I guess I was nervous. Meeting with a group of people that I had considered my adversaries off and on through the years had a tendency to make me feel uncomfortable. Jan and I sat down, and after a little bit of small talk, I got right to the point. "We've been feeling like maybe our time here is coming to a close," I said.

I think it caught some of them by surprise. I had tried very hard to fit into the farm way of life and strived to be an asset, but I knew it was time for a change. I can't remember what all was said. The only remark that really sticks out in my mind was one said by Michael O' Dowd. He had been a Jesuit priest prior to getting involved with the Move, and his people skills left a lot to be desired. As we all sat in the stillness of the room, absorbing my announcement, he blurted out, "Well, it's probably good that you go. You don't take part in the meetings, you don't sing, you don't do devotions. You're a blemish on the farm."

In the few seconds that followed, you could have heard a pin drop. I think what he said took everyone by surprise. Several people stared at the floor, shuffling their feet and

Chapter Twenty-Eight

clearing their throats. Without saying a word, Jan got up and went downstairs. I heard the door open and slam shut with such force that the whole building shook.

There wasn't a lot more to say. Someone asked when we would be leaving, and I told them early spring, if that was okay. Winter isn't a very good time to be making a major move. I let them know that I would be retaining our entire permanent fund, as we were going to need it to live on until we got established. After a little more small talk, I left.

When I got home, I could tell Jan had been crying. We had invested 10 years into the farm, through good times and bad. To be told you were a blemish was pretty much a slap in the face. Of course, Michael was just referring to me when he said that, but we both felt the impact of his stinging words. We talked a bit and heard someone come up the stairs and knock on the door. It was Bob Cramer. He had been promoted to the eldership several years before and had been in the meeting we'd just left.

"Can I come in?" he asked quietly.

"Sure, Bob. Come on in," I said. From his demeanor, I knew he was troubled by what had happened.

He sat in a chair and looked at the floor for a few seconds before speaking. "Hey, I'm sorry that happened. After you left, we all climbed on Michael and let him know how inappropriate that was. He was speaking for himself, not the whole eldership."

I can't remember much of what was said after that. My mind was a blur. Though I knew that I'd had my run-ins with the elders, I'd never considered myself to be a black sheep. The words that had been spoken hurt deeply, but there wasn't much to be done about it now. I appreciated Bob coming over and just being a friend. The next day, I went to the office in the tabernacle and told Michael he owed Jan an apology, which he agreed to.

The eldership offered us $500 for the woodstove and

Wilderness Blues

washing machine. We thought about it for a bit and reluctantly agreed to accept the offer. They were getting a bargain, but I didn't want to pack those things into town.

As for the house, as per the resident's agreement, we had to relinquish ownership. Another family moved to the farm a few years later and was given our home to live in. They had the option of paying us for the materials that we'd purchased, but opted not to. Needless to say, they weren't my favorite folks.

In February of 1987, we moved into Hoonah. We packed all of our furniture, clothes and tools into a 22-foot skiff and left Mt. Bether, after 10 1/2 years. Leaving was kind of bittersweet. For years, I had longed for this day, and now that it was here, I had reservations. It was like graduating from high school, leaving all that was familiar behind. I was launching out into the deep with no safety net, and this time, I was dragging eight other people with me. I was scared of failure, but there was no turning back now.

We moved into a house that was being rented by some friends who had previously left the farm and were going south for a few months. After they returned, we lived at the parsonage of the Assembly of God church with the pastor and his family. There were even a few weeks that we had to move back to the farm while we were waiting for the house we were buying to become available. It was unsettling, but it all worked out.

In a small town like Hoonah, it's almost impossible to avoid people. I was working at L. Kane's and came in contact with various members of the farm on a fairly regular basis. We were polite to each other when we met, but were unwilling or unable to bond. Living at the farm was the one thing that we'd all had in common. I had been a part of them and was no more. We were no longer part of the first fruits company, and though things have changed dramatically since our exodus, the feeling at the time was that we

Chapter Twenty-Eight

were deceived. Somehow, because we were no longer on the farm or in the Move, we weren't quite up to par, spiritually. We were considered to be in the outer court, a place made up of worldly people and unbelievers. It made for some awkward moments for those first few years.

For a long time after we left, I harbored some bitter feelings. I didn't think it was right to turn people loose from these farms without concern for their welfare. It seemed to go against Christian standards. I didn't like the feeling of superiority when I was on the farm, and I disliked it even more when we left. I'd sat through enough meetings to know the mindset of the ministry regarding those who were not in the Move and didn't care to be on the receiving end of that way of thinking. When people asked me questions about the farm, I had little good to say about it, rehearsing over and over all that I'd found wrong with it. Though I was no longer a part of Mt. Bether, they still occupied territory in my mind. It took a few years, but gradually, the anger and hurt began to dissolve.

The changes that had begun on the farm when we were still there were apparently continuing. Perhaps it was the mass exodus of so many people, or maybe it was just an understanding that the status quo wasn't working, I don't know. A few years after we left, I started sensing a friendlier atmosphere around my former colleagues when we had chance meetings in town. Many of the elders who had ruled the camp when we lived there had moved on, so maybe that had something to do with the new attitude. In any event, the barrier that was once between us seemed to be melting away.

On more than one occasion, Bob Cramer helped me fix something on my boat, and I was able to reciprocate. It was a good feeling to be working together again, even if only for a few hours. The cold war appeared to be over, and I, for one, was glad.

Chapter Twenty-Nine

I'm not sure who all came and went during the time that we lived at Game Creek. Jason Simms (the only black man at the farm) kept a record of such things until 1983. I guess that's the year that he left. From 1975 until 1983, 172 people called Mt. Bether at Game Creek home. 22 men and women held the title of elder during that time span, though at one convention, several people who had been set into the eldership were later given the position of deacon (a presumably lower place). 25 children were born to parents who lived at the farm. There were two sets of twins. Five people died; one was a baby – I believe it was stillborn – and another was a young man who left the farm to pursue a more liberal lifestyle and later died in a car accident in California. He was held up as an example of what could happen to those who rebelled. Three men perished on one day in July, 1978, in a terrible boating accident. One of them was John Borelli, the elder who was in charge of the transportation for the farm. I don't remember hearing any explanation as to why they died, though I'm sure the reason was more natural than spiritual, since they were out on a day when the water was really rough.

There were 11 weddings performed at the farm. Three ended in divorce, though not while the couples were at Mt. Bether. One marriage lasted less than a year – the newlywed was one of the men killed in the boating accident.

In 1979, the school produced its first graduates. There was a total of 13 recorded in the Chronicles of Game Creek. All have long since left the farm. One of them succumbed to a disease that he'd had since he was a child. To the best of my knowledge, the rest are healthy and successful in their lives.

The farm is still in existence. I haven't been out there for

Wilderness Blues

a few years. I didn't return for a visit the first time until 10 years had passed. I guess I was still harboring some bitter feelings. The last time I was there was for a memorial service for an old family friend. The buildings were looking a little rundown at the time. Some of them have been around for almost 30 years though. When they were erected, no one thought the world would last this long. Who knew?

I'm not sure how many people live there now, but I believe that there are less than 25. I think most of the young people have moved on. I spoke to one young couple recently; they are debating whether to put their limited funds into the cabin they live in or save their money for a down payment on a house in town. The husband is approaching 30, and has been on the farm all of his life. He and his wife will have to face the decision of what to do with their lives soon.

Of the 172 people listed in the Chronicles, only 10 remain at the farm. I've spoken to a few of them on several occasions, wondering what their plans are. By and large, they intend to remain at Game Creek. It's not an easy life. While things have gotten better down through the years, it's still no picnic. Everyone is getting older, and even with a healthy lifestyle, there are limits to what a body can do.

There is a logging road that runs close by, so they don't have to take a boat home anymore, but once they reach the end of the road, they have to walk a mile or so across a small creek and through woods and fields that the bears claim as their own. They still take a barge to town and fill up an old fuel truck to run the generator and farm machinery. As far as I know, outhouses are yet the norm, though with fewer people, they probably don't fill up as fast.

I wonder what will happen when there are no more young people to run things, to plow the fields or milk the cows or renovate buildings in need of repair. I wonder and I care, but it's out of my hands.

Chapter Thirty

At one time, Mt. Bether pursued an isolationist point of view, as did all the farms in the Move. There was an elitist air about the farm that became a barrier between the outside world and Game Creek. An "us versus them" mentality separated the farm from the rest of society, and that's the way they wanted it. I don't believe it's that way anymore. A few years ago, the farm purchased a tackle shop in town and has grown it into a thriving business, largely because of the service they give. I've become good friends with the people who are running it and have even had an opportunity to work with them on a few occasions. This past year, I once again fished for halibut with Bob Cramer in what proved to be a mutually satisfying and profitable trip.

For the past four or five years, the folks at Game Creek have extended an invitation to the whole town to join them in a Thanksgiving celebration at the farm. It's been well received by everyone and has served to break down any barriers that may have existed.

Not long ago, I ran into Michael O'Dowd on a Web site devoted to people who used to be in the Move. When I saw his name, I had mixed emotions, remembering our last encounter at the elders' meeting. I decided to write anyway and was pleasantly surprised when he wrote back and apologized for not being a good shepherd while at the farm. I told Jan about it, and it made us both feel good. It was nice to close that chapter in our lives.

Jan and I recently had dinner with some good friends who had been with us at Game Creek. I was lamenting the time lost while we were there, the hardships we endured and the religious baloney that we believed at one time. He looked at me and said, "Well, you know, Tom, if it hadn't been for the farm, you probably wouldn't have come to

Chapter Thirty

Alaska, you wouldn't have a fishing boat, and you wouldn't know us. Here, have another potato."

What more could be said? As I reached for another spud, I realized he was right. Something good comes from everything. The trials we endured have made strong bonds between those of us who used to call Game Creek home. If I spent 10 years on a farm in the Alaskan wilderness for no other reason than to gain the friendship of so many fine people, then it was time well spent. Nonetheless, if I had to do it over again, I don't know that I would.

References

Hoonah Public School, Alaska History Class 1973. *Hoonah History.*

Orth, Donald J. 1967. *Dictionary of Alaska Place Names.* United States Government Printing Office, Washington.

Smith, Jacob. *The Chronicles of Game Creek: From 1975-1983.*